Black Coffee and Red Lipstick

Notes on Living

Alexandra
Shulman

Black Coffee and Red Lipstick

Notes on Living

MITCHELL BEAZLEY

First published in Great Britain in 2026
by Mitchell Beazley, an imprint of
Octopus Publishing Group Ltd, Carmelite House,
50 Victoria Embankment, London EC4Y 0DZ
www.octopusbooks.co.uk

An Hachette UK Company
www.hachette.co.uk

The authorized representative in the EEA is Hachette Ireland,
8 Castlecourt Centre, Dublin 15, D15 XTP3, Ireland
email: info@hbgi.ie

Distributed in the US by Hachette Book Group,
1290 Avenue of the Americas, 4th and 5th Floors, New York, NY 10104

Distributed in Canada by Canadian Manda Group
664 Annette St., Toronto, Ontario, Canada M6S 2C8

ISBN: 978-1-84601-778-0
eISBN: 978-1-84601-781-0

A CIP catalogue record for this book is available from the British Library.

Printed and bound in Great Britain

10 9 8 7 6 5 4 3 2 1

Publishing Director: Alison Starling
Creative Director: Jonathan Christie
Senior Editor: Alex Stetter
Editorial Assistant: Annie Bowes
Senior Production Manager: Katherine Hockley

For my mother, Drusilla

1927–2026

Contents

Introduction

This book began life in a tent at the Dubai International Hotel during the 2023 Book Festival. A woman approached me with a copy of my earlier book – also a series of essays, *Clothes...and Other Things That Matter* – to be signed and told me she had worked at the National Portrait Gallery when I was a trustee there and that when she left her long career, she felt lost. She didn't know what to do. She didn't really know who she was.

Having left my 25-year career at *Vogue* a few years previously, I understood what she was saying and we briefly discussed the issue of finding oneself a new life. When you are used to living a certain kind of existence, it can be difficult to work out exactly what you are interested in, how you want to spend your days. You aren't entirely sure how the person that you have been is going to adapt and mould itself to a different existence, nor what that existence might be.

Black Coffee and Red Lipstick – Notes on Living was triggered by that conversation and subsequent thoughts about the things that make us the person we are, the person we once were and the person we might become. Some change, some remain an indelible part of us.

Since leaving *Vogue* in 2017, I have gone through several major life experiences: two different cancers, the death of my mother and, more joyfully, a second marriage. Each has had a massive effect on the way I view life. There is less certainty, perhaps more acceptance. There is a new value in contentment, but also a desire to appreciate as much as possible. A keener awareness of what the smaller things bring to our life. Yes, black coffee, but also the pleasure of a picnic, the continuing delight in a snowy night, the comfort of roast chicken. These essays range around all of the above as well as some less straightforward thoughts: on wearing white trousers in winter, time spent alone, the pain and delight of being in love.

It was these aspects of life that I wanted to write about and explore. The world in 2026 is a febrile space filled with questions about identity politics, gender, race, political dissonance, populism, the fear of immigration and the progress of wars. This book does not attempt to address those issues in any direct way. Not because I am not interested in them or unaware of the effect they have, but simply because they are not the subjects I wanted to write about, nor do I feel qualified to add great insight to those debates.

Instead the book is a mixture of memoir, anecdote, social observation and cultural history, drawing on my personal experience as a child, a journalist, a young woman always looking for the great love, a mother, a magazine editor and now a woman in the liminal space between middle and old age.

My big thoughts are on small things, things that aren't always simple or uncomplicated or fair. They won't be everyone's preoccupations, but hopefully they will inspire readers to consider their personal world and the pillars that make them who they are, even if everything around them is constantly changing.

Black Coffee and Red Lipstick – Notes on Living is no self-help book. It provides few, if any, straight answers and asks a lot of questions. Just like life, really.

Do You Remember the Second Time?

How easy it would be if, when we find something we love, we could just experience it again and again and discover the same degree of satisfaction.

My partner David and I were sitting in The White Cat, a whitewashed taverna on the Greek island of Poros, gazing out over the calm, sparkling blue of the sea lapping just beyond our feet. We had eaten a late lunch there the previous day and found it so delightful that it was an easy decision to return.

For that first lunch, we had sat at a table bordering the water, looking out to the main town across the bay. The restaurant was relatively empty, with only a couple of other tables occupied. This time we were seated next to a multi-generational party at a big table. Nothing the matter with that. It added a different element to the spot and it was interesting to try to work out whether it was a birthday or a christening or just a big family get-together. People-watching is part of the delight of restaurants.

We studied the menu the waitress brought to the table. Filled with Greek classics, there was nothing experimental or modern Greek about what was on offer, which was part of the appeal. Although we looked down the predictable list of hummus, grilled halloumi, spicy sausages, meatballs, stuffed vine leaves, chicken souvlaki, red mullet *et al.*, we already knew what we were going to have. We'd enjoyed the meal the day before so much, we both ordered the same as we had then. For me, a Cretan salad of harsh rusk bread soaked in olive oil, herbs and tomatoes, while David had his favourite *melitzanosalata*, a puree of aubergine, garlic, parsley and lemon with warm pitta bread, followed by a bowl of steamed mussels.

On this second outing, despite being seemingly identical in every way, the meal was not nearly as good. Was it the taste? Was it the presentation? What was it? The olive oil in my salad tasted a touch less peppery, the soaked bread was a fraction too mushy and the tomatoes somehow less... It was all fine, but it was all just less. Had it tasted like that the first time, we probably wouldn't have repeated our order. We might well have thought we would try something else. And that is so often the way when you order on repeat. The specialness of the first experience will never be replicated.

'Do you remember the first time?' sings Pulp's Jarvis

Cocker, a man who still manages to make corduroy suits look cool and make the words resonate, even though he is now in his sixties with a greying beard. In that 1994 song, he tries to persuade a past lover to be unfaithful to her current, dull boyfriend, even though that first time with her, quite possibly his first time with anyone, was clearly not particularly successful. 'I can't remember a worse time,' he follows up. But it was highly memorable. Sex is an excellent example of something that is not necessarily brilliant the first time – but all the same you are unlikely to forget it. First kisses, on the other hand – and this may not be an opinion shared by everyone – can be shockingly good and never bettered.

The second time of anything very, very rarely has that same quality. It fails to make a mark and frequently disappoints. Take clothes buying. How easy it would be if, when we find something we love, we could just buy it again and again and discover the same degree of satisfaction. But second time around, I never get that same hit of the pleasure of discovery and knowing I've scored a bullseye with my choice.

There are people I know who happily trade the excitement of discovery when buying clothes for ease and convenience. They have no interest in spending their time truffling out something completely new and different. And very often, but not exclusively, they are men.

A few summers ago, I stayed in a house up in the Hollywood Hills, where the road wound up from Sunset Boulevard, past the famous Chateau Marmont hotel, past electronic gates guarding expensive properties. There was a huge, almost impossibly green lawn at the back maintained by a rigorous regime of sprinklers. The first few days of our visit, the view of the city spread below was often covered by the marine layer, the fog caused by the warm air passing over the cold water of the Pacific. Eventually it lifted and then you got the money shot – the whole city reaching to the ocean, the sparkling grid of the streets and moving cars like an illuminated ticker tape on the freeways at night.

Our host was a charismatic LA producer, evoked by Joni Mitchell in her song 'Ladies' Man' on the *Wild Things Run Fast* album and to some small degree immortalized by a line which compares his love for her with his love for cocaine – the latter being more overwhelming. In his substantial wardrobe, shelves were stacked with near-identical pale grey needlecord trousers, and similarly identical white shirts. He suited this stylish, relaxed yet deliberate uniform. It wasn't as rigid a look as the black turtlenecks that Steve Jobs famously wore every day, but it was a uniform all the same. I never asked him what his first experience of grey needlecord had been, an experience that had led him to buy them again and again.

You might think that realizing the risk involved in buying clothes on repeat would ring an alarm bell when I'm shopping, but life isn't that simple. How often have I found what I considered to be a great pair of trousers and then bought a second identical pair, only to realize when they arrived that they just didn't feel as good? Why, despite multiple attempts, can I never find the James Perse T shirt that I first bought, which had just the right neckline? They all look the same, but somehow they aren't.

Recently I came across some cotton, barrel-leg trousers in a boutique in Lafayette, Louisiana. They were fantastic. Were they so fantastic because I discovered them in this little place stuffed with brands I had never heard of, right opposite a bar delivering great margaritas? Or were they just exactly what I wanted to wear at that moment? Whatever it was, I came back to London and started obsessing about them, wondering whether, if they were so great, I should try and find them in another colour.

So I did my research and discovered they were by Le Bon Shoppe, an LA brand, and were available at several places in the UK, including a shopping centre in King's Cross. That did remove a touch of their lustre – when you return home with something you have bought in Louisiana, you don't really want to discover it is available just a few miles up the road. Be that as it may, I pressed 'buy' on my screen and scooped up another pair. There were a pale denim, dark denim, black, khaki and ecru all available. I went for the ecru. They fitted OK and looked pleasant, but... pleasant isn't enough. The thrill had gone.

I did the same with a pair of hugely expensive Balenciaga trainers a few years back, the most expensive trainers I had ever bought in my life. I was in Athens in a sudden heavy thunderstorm and the nearest shelter was the Balenciaga store. I had never considered buying a pair of Balenciaga trainers, nor in fact any trainers costing £395, but these were irresistible. Delicious, polished white leather mixed with mesh, with a black grosgrain band across the slightly pointed toe. Eventually they became grubby, and grubby white Balenciaga trainers do not look as they should. So I bought another pair, hoping I would feel the same way about them. I didn't. It was a couple of years later and perhaps the shape had changed incrementally, but they didn't have that special quality that meant even my local dry cleaner complimented me on them.

It's similar to the second album or second novel syndrome. Being successful in the repeat buying of a T shirt is not the same as having to follow up a first-time bestseller like Harper Lee's *To Kill a Mockingbird*, but there's a similarity. But you'll only know after going in for the second time whether it's possible to achieve the memorable thrill of the first time.

Red Lipstick

***Fact:** I would like to be the kind of person who wears red lipstick.*
***Fact:** I only rarely succeed.*

I have always admired women who wear red lipstick and have frequently attempted to be one of them. The dash of colour delivers so much, not only in how it looks but in what it says. I also have huge respect for those who wear their lipstick with a naturalness that implies it is simply the case that they were, of course, going to apply their lipstick every morning, every evening. And this is relevant because, no matter how much 'long-lasting' blurb the brand claims, red lipstick needs to be immaculate and this requires constant reapplication. Which means that the red lipstick wearer must always be conscious of their lips and the way they look. At my school, one headmistress advised anyone considering doing any public speaking to wear lipstick so that the audience could see our mouths as we put our case forward.

A few months ago, I was having dinner in a Portuguese

restaurant in one of the strange spaces that have now taken over central London. Where once there were streets and buildings, now there are massive craters and cranes behind hoardings. It's disorientating when so many of the familiar landmarks have disappeared.

Andrea was sitting at the table and, along with a green silk, Mao-collared shirt, she was wearing a glorious fuchsia shade of lipstick which didn't seem to shift even after she had drunk a white port with tonic and dug into several of the fried croquettes. I have never seen her without lipstick. I asked her what it was and she showed me a Dior colour, 777 in a red tube. I don't think she wears any other make-up. It's her mouth you notice.

When did she start to wear red lipstick? 'When I began to work in Albania' was the unexpected answer. 'In Albania, all women wear red lipstick. You look very plain without it. And so I thought I should wear it too.' Albanian women, she told me, love to dress up, a little like Italian women are often thought to do, with an overtly sexy and colourful style. They see no worth in a black trouser suit. But red lipstick is another thing. Red lipstick is part of the equipment of life in a country that has been through bleak, demanding, difficult times.

It's important to define red, because anyone who wants

to wear red lipstick has first to work out their particular red. It is so obvious, so attention drawing and so deliberate that there must be no mistake.

Red has range. It travels from light to dark through boundaries that leach into pink, purple, brown, orange. It is, in spite of this, a colour that most people can agree on, unlike blue or green, which can confuse some, such as the man I live with. 'Shall I wear this shirt or this one?' he will ask, pulling out a blue one and a white one. I say, 'That one,' gesturing at the one which is clearly blue. 'The green one?' he asks, to which I reply that there is no green in the mix, only blue and white. He sees no blue. So there we go. One person's green or blue is most certainly not another's.

Red, by contrast, is far less likely to provoke uncertainty. There is nothing uncertain about red. It is the only colour that has the same determined clarity as black and white. It is uplifting and threatening. As the colour of blood, it is and always has been powerful. It is used to draw attention because it stands out. There's a reason why it is the most commonly used colour on national flags – around 75 per cent of them. It says 'Look at me.' It says 'STOP.'

So mess with red lipstick at your peril. Get it right and it is one of the most gloriously effective tools. Get it wrong and it can detonate your whole look.

In the attempt to become a red lipstick wearer, I have spent several thoroughly enjoyable yet ultimately relatively fruitless hours watching lipstick tutorials on YouTube from the make-up artist and beauty entrepreneur Lisa Eldridge. She has one specifically for red lipstick. I have discovered that, to avoid emphasizing the downturn at the side of the mouth, the trick is to apply a concealer at the corner, where there is a crease that runs beyond the lip line. You don't want the colour to bleed into this troublesome gully. I watch Lisa, and several other make-up gurus, create mouths that have no creases or irregularity, where the colour is even, flat, velvety or shiny.

Red lipstick is something to wear throughout life – although, like many things that make you stand out, it is harder to have the confidence for it as you age. But in fact it is one of those small items that can make a huge difference to your face, and to the way people consider you. You are a woman who wears red lipstick, someone not at all invisible or wanting to loiter in the shadows.

Shortly before leaving *Vogue,* I became intrigued by the red lipstick I had so admired on others and the beauty team arranged for Justine Jenkins, a leading make-up artist, to come to my office to give me a lesson on how to wear it. This is where I learned the calculus of red lipsticks, on a chart Justine had drawn with little daubs of colour. These included:

— 13 warm reds
— 7 blue reds
— 6 neutral reds
— 7 pink reds
— 6 brick reds
— 7 wine reds

These were then multiplied by textures, balms, gloss, matts, satins, stains. It became an extremely complex and fascinating spreadsheet.

On me, a pink red comes out more tomato in one texture than in another. A brick red appears substantially more pink on my skin. The blue reds which I expected to drain my face of colour actually brighten it. The wine reds make me look like Count Dracula's grandmother.

I noticed that while the colour does draw attention to my mouth, it also affects the eyes, oddly making them more vibrant, a point Rachel Felder draws attention to in her book *Red Lipstick*, dedicated to the subject: she writes that 'it makes both pale and dark eyes sparkle'. After several hours of tuition, I came away with seven options which I was excited to try out. And now, years later, I am still experimenting.

Where once red lipstick was seen as a deliberate indicator of wanting to appear sexually attractive, that era of the red-lipsticked vamp has long gone. Red lipstick now is seen not as anything to do with appealing to men, but as a sign of empowerment, of being the woman you want to be and saying what you want to say. The American Democratic politician Alexandria Ocasio-Cortez is known for her lipstick, along with her vigorously left-of-centre politics. Amal Clooney addresses both courts of human rights and film award ceremonies unashamedly wearing hers. The novelist Zadie Smith usually wears a vivid red lipstick when she speaks on race and age and writing. Queen Elizabeth II always wore a pretty deep red that stood out against her extraordinarily youthful skin and white hair. These women are not quiet. They have something to say (even the late queen, although she mostly kept her thoughts private).

Currently, I have 15 red lipsticks in my dressing table, a mix of matt tubes, lip liners, colour enhancers and lip balms. There are four Chanel Rouge Coco lipsticks, Tom Ford's Scarlet Rouge (incidentally a disaster on my skin colour, but I love the packaging), Giorgio Armani Rouge

Ecstasy, Dior Addict Strawberry Lip Glow, Charlotte Tilbury's Red Carpet Red, Hourglass Raven. In the final days of writing this book, I escaped to buy a tube of Violette_FR Pomme d'Amour Bisou Jelly. When in need of some support, a new lipstick is an excellent option.

Some days one shade will suit me better than another. Some days none will work. Today, for example, I am writing with a thick head cold and to apply red lipstick seems an impossibility. I could no more wear red lipstick than I could plunge into a freezing-cold pond. Instead of being endowed with positivity and power, I would feel diminished by it. Other days it's like an injection of bravado, in its own way a magical power, like a superhero's cape.

It packs a huge punch for such a small object. There are few things in life so easily available, portable, inexpensive and transformative as a beautiful bullet of red lipstick.

The Mother

Perhaps all women feel this way, but I have never thought of myself as the mother.

My mother was alive when I began working on this book. She was still living in our childhood home and, although increasingly immobile, was in remarkably good form for her age – then 96. She completely understood what I was hoping to achieve, even though I was pretty inarticulate about what that was. We talked about possible titles and approaches to the cover. The knowledge that she thought it was a good idea – and she by no means thought everything I did was a good idea – was a huge encouragement. I had hoped she might still be around to see it published, but she died nine months before.

As she became more housebound, I would often take over dinner – something easy to heat up in her 1950s-style gas oven; a ready-made risotto or fish pie. And she would have asked me on the phone before I arrived if she should make her salad dressing, to which I invariably answered yes, as it was an exceptionally good vinaigrette that I have never managed to replicate.

The dressing would be sitting in the base of the Perspex salad bowl that she had come to use, replacing the large wooden one she used when we ate as a family, waiting for lettuce, tomatoes and cucumber to be added. And then the salad would have to be tossed, an activity she took immensely seriously. One evening I commented impatiently that she spent a crazy amount of time tossing the salad. After that, at each of these suppers she would say briskly before sitting down, 'Alexandra, now I expect *you* would like to toss the salad.' It was when she stopped delivering this only partially joking admonition that I knew she was fading.

We would eat at the dining table, the same table where most of my teenage suppers had been eaten, and talk about every member of the family, in particular her five grandchildren; about her frustration at being enfeebled; and about my professional life. 'How goes it at the *Mail*?' she would ask of the paper which had been publishing my weekly column for several years. 'What news at the *Telegraph*?' she would ask of the paper where she was last employed for 18 years.

As she became weaker, some days the conversation was more difficult and often repetitious, her memory failing to record something one had said a few minutes before. Sometimes she had a particular concern about a member of the family that it was impossible to assuage – frequently they were not serious matters – and the issue went round and round on an unbreakable loop. She was convinced that she lived with three ghosts and would sometimes point one of them out in the corner of the sitting room where she spent most of her days, or above the fireplace. She had reached an accommodation with them and didn't mind them being there in the slightest.

But her judgement and conversation on many matters remained completely sound. She could talk about an artist or a writer with staggering clarity and perception. She remained passionate about what she was interested in – in her last year, this included the growth of the Nazi movement in Germany, David Attenborough's programmes and anything she could read about the sinking of the *Titanic*.

I'm writing this on the first Easter Sunday she is no longer alive. She died 38 days ago. Easter was one of her maternal strongpoints. She was never one for those elaborate Easter tables with furry ducklings and floral arrangements and baskets of eggs, but for years when we were children, she organized magnificent Easter-egg hunts in various rented holiday homes in the English countryside.

With the help of our father, she would hide industrial quantities of miniature foil-covered chocolate eggs around the gardens while we were shut indoors on sentence of death if we peeked. The eggs were perched on branches, balanced on the sturdier petals and leaves, tucked into corners and lodged in stone walls and brickwork.

Usually there were enough hunters to be divided into two teams and, hoping to avoid the catastrophe that would occur if one child ended up with fewer eggs than another, the contents of each of our buckets were to be put into the two communal team buckets near the house and then shared out so everyone ended up with an equal number. It never worked out quite like that since, human nature being what it is, and particularly well demonstrated by the under-fives, everyone ate some of the ones they found on the way, or hid them about their person for later. Even now, 60 years later, I remember the delight of seeing a pink- or green-foiled miniature egg glinting out of the garden wall, days after the hunt was over.

This remained the inspiration for the Easter-egg hunts that both my sister and I would organize in years to come. Today, I am acutely missing our mother, knowing that if she were still alive, she would have an egg for me. No longer a hunt, but still a commemorative egg.

To me she had remained the mother in the family, even when in recent years she was unable to fulfil much of the role that one expects mothers to fulfil – other than the most important one, an unconditional love. But then, during her decades of mothering, she didn't take part in many of the activities lots of women chose to. She was never the woman teaching us how to bake, or overseeing our homework, or connecting with the families of our school friends. She would never have wanted to be on a class WhatsApp or involved in some kind of transport rota for extracurricular sport. She didn't play board games with us or, as far as I remember, bath us at night. Going through her papers, it appeared that her advice to other young mothers wondering how to juggle work and motherhood was: 'I hardly ever look at the crib.'

As we became adults, she would converse with us, her children, as she would with anyone else. We, like her, had all made careers in journalism, writing and art, and she had strong opinions on what we were doing, either delighted by our work or sometimes critical.

She wanted to be involved in any part of any social life we had, enjoying the company of our generation of friends as much as – perhaps more than – her own. Yet despite the lack of traditional maternal behaviour during much of our lives, she was always the mother in the family.

She was physically affectionate and always delighted to see or hear from any of us once we were no longer living at home with her. She took Christmas and birthdays seriously – even when very ill, she would be distraught at the idea she might have missed giving us a gift. She wanted to think of herself as someone who could sort out our problems in any way she possibly could and when she was confined to her home, even to one chair, she would still always ask, 'What can I do to help?' Like many mothers, she hated the idea that she could not be of use. She was our unreserved cheerleader right to the end.

I don't know if it is because of her, or perhaps all women feel this way, but I have never thought of myself as *the* mother, even though I have given birth and brought up a child. I became *a* mother the second my son Sam was born. As soon as I saw him, I recognized him as someone utterly familiar – and I knew that this was a person I was going to care passionately for, all my life. From the moment I first held him, I couldn't imagine how I could bear not to be with him. How would I ever trust he was safe without being in my presence? The notion that I would have to be back in my office after my three months' maternity leave was terrifying and incomprehensible. How would I survive the days when I wasn't able to watch his every movement?

Yet despite that unassailable attachment, when I read the mountains of prose and polemic written around the issue of motherhood, I feel an outsider. Somebody who is looking curiously in on an experience rather than experiencing it. I listen with interest but a degree of incomprehension to young women discussing their small children's tiniest developmental stages – tummy time, napping hours, sleep training – while knowing that at no point did I engage with these issues in that same forensic way. There are so many mothers who track every aspect of their child's existence, themselves fuelled by their small successes and anxious about their failures in a way I don't think I ever was. Some of that is simply a changing culture, but I can't imagine joining in a Mumsnet debate on any subject; and often, when I listen to a programme like *Women's Hour* discussing some aspect of motherhood, I wonder whether I was deficient in not having the same engagement in so many aspects of my son's young life.

It wasn't as if I didn't very, very much want to be a mother. At 37, I was relatively old to be giving birth for the first time. Many of my friends and many of the women I worked with were already mothers two, three, four times over. It wasn't that I had a particular fondness for babies or children but, although I was never particularly sure about many things – my career, for example, or my love life – I was 100 per cent sure that I wanted a child. Now I wonder why that was. What was the urge to have this baby?

This was in the mid-1990s and, although it would have been possible to have a child alone, that was a far rarer decision then than it is nowadays. Not just that to embark on it solo is entirely socially acceptable today, but with great advances in fertility treatments and also the ability to freeze our eggs, it is far more possible. But although this baby was something I wanted desperately, I never considered taking that route. I was involved in a fairly on/off relationship with a man who, though he loved me, already had two children and didn't feel he could manage another one. I was aware that if I became pregnant, it could be a catastrophe and I would have to go it alone, something I wasn't confident that I would be able to manage. Who knows what the 36-year-old me would have done nowadays when women having children on their own is far more common?

When I discovered I was pregnant, only a couple of months after that man and I eventually married, it was simply wonderful. Both he and I were besotted with this unborn child. It's possible that I never felt more maternal than I did when our son was still in the womb and I carried him with me every second of the day, and worried about him almost as often. If worrying about one's child is a sign of motherhood, I definitely qualify, since even now, 31 years later, my default position is that there is always something to worry about. 'What's up?' I answer his calls with, hoping it sounds like general interest but knowing he reads it correctly as 'What should I be worrying about?' I hear our relationship reflected in one of my father's favourite Jewish jokes, about a Jewish mother's telegram to her son: 'Letter following STOP Start worrying STOP.'

Talking to a therapist about motherhood after the death of my mother, they pointed out that I talk of *the* mother. As if there is only one. And yes, that's true. *The* mother is my mother. I am not *the* mother. It's possible, now that she is no longer alive and there is an emptiness where she once was, that this might change. Perhaps I will become *the* mother, but I really doubt it.

A Friendship Wardrobe

Just as we don't consider one item to be able to come riding in on a charger for every event, neither should we expect the same of friends.

In the summer of 2013, the paperback edition of *My Brilliant Friend*, the first of Elena Ferrante's Neapolitan quartet, was published in the UK. The cover of the book, with its picture of a bride and groom followed by three young girls, could be seen everywhere: on the Tube, beside beds, on sun loungers. This tale of friendship between Elena and Lila, set in the frequently violent and brutal 1950s Naples, was devoured, primarily by women of all ages, and sold over 15 million copies worldwide.

I never managed to complete the book which so many people loved, but I read enough of it to grasp that it was a powerful excavation of friendship, an area that, with the vast range of emotionally complex issues involved, is such a rich subject for fiction.

Friendship is such a strong feature of our lives, so layered and nuanced and utterly dependent on such a wide variety of factors that, to deal with the vast array of what is required, a friendship wardrobe is needed.

In a perfect world, our wardrobe contains clothes suitable for all manner of occasions and moods. Just as we don't consider one item to be able to come riding in on a charger for every event, neither should we expect the same of friends. There is no one-size-fits-all approach when it comes to friends and, unlike our clothes, they can't usually be dressed up or down or styled in five different ways to make them adaptable to different circumstances.

They are, more often, very much suited to specific purposes. Not so much an interchangeable selection of denim, white T shirts and basic black trousers as an array of memorable evening dresses, bikinis, a dressing gown and the treasured expensive item that we pull on year after year because we know we look good in it and have a good time when we're wearing it. Not that we always have a good time with our friends. Curiously, in *Roget's Thesaurus*, there is no satisfactory alternative for the word friend. Benefactor, colleague, crony, acquaintance, kind person – these are not the same as friends. Or not to me, but perhaps to others they qualify.

As they are for many people, my childhood and teenage years were all about my friends. I was fortunate. I was good at making friends, a term which in itself suggests there is some skill in the achievement, but if there is, it's not one I have ever been aware of. I never remember fearing not being picked by a team leader to be on their team in whatever game we played in the playground or park. This wasn't because I was any good at the game, but because I was considered a friend.

Over the years, there have been lost friends whom I regret and new friends who have added completely different elements to my world. It's clear, though, that even the closest friends are only able to fulfil a certain number of demands at any one time.

We need friends for amusement and entertainment, for consolation, for advice, for company, for emotional support. I want to be able to gossip with them about other friends over supper, to talk with them for hours on the phone trying to avoid work, to share holidays and to have them understand my long-established family relationships. But I also want to have friends in my wardrobe who know little about my history – which allows them an objective distance that can at times be crucial.

In the ideal world in which most of us do not live, there would be one or two friends who could fulfil all these requirements. But that's not the way things are. Not only is one person unable to answer all our needs, but friendship is shapeshifting. It's not the sturdy, reliable structure it would be nice to think it is, but something that is constantly evolving at the whim of circumstance, place, time and other people. The friendship wardrobe allows for the fact that friends are not adaptable, since they often aren't, but has people *in situ* to slot in for whatever we want.

My oldest friend and I met at the age of seven at my first term at junior school, yet she is not the person I turn to in many situations. Over the years, we have spent time in different countries, had romantic lives that the other was less a part of and differing careers. But I still think of her as my best friend and she thinks the same of me.

She has been the most formative friend in my life, introducing me to people I would never have known without her, including the man I am married to. But we have frequently been like trams, moving alongside each other on the line, then being diverted in different directions and on the return journey finding ourselves again side by side in the depot.

I can't imagine a world that doesn't contain her, but even so I can't think of a single occasion when she has dropped everything to be with me, nor I her. On hearing I had been told my mother was dying, she didn't ask about her or how I was feeling, but instead invited me to a dinner she was planning that week. My mother was still alive that night of the dinner and I went and had, as always, the entertaining and amusing time my friend so often provides, escaping for a few hours the miserable concerns that were my constant companion at that time. That's what she does. And it has been invaluable over the years.

So she occupies a certain role in the friendship wardrobe of people who have not been deliberately put together but accumulated by default. It's not as if we need to acquire a new friend who likes playing tennis and go out looking for them as if they were a pair of ankle boots.

Naturally, over the years, there have been some I have discarded or who have discarded me, and others from school days or university who have re-emerged decades later and who it was instantly easy to engage with, each returning as the familiar characters we were when we first met. And there have been others, now hugely important, who have come into my life through work or chance acquaintance. One of my top tips in life is to continue to make new friends.

This might sound straightforward, but as people age, they can atrophy in the friendship stakes. As with all wardrobes, we will always benefit from some new input. The patterns that become ingrained with old friends don't exist with new. We don't expect them to behave in a certain way.

In fact, with new friends there are no expectations of any kind. They also see us in an entirely different way to old friends. They know nothing about the baggage we haul around, they haven't been part of the existing rivalries and pecking order of an established friendship group. We can spend time with them and actually escape ourselves in a way that is exhilarating. One friend was told that she always placed her shiny new friends on the front of the shelf and shunted the older, dusty ones to the back, no longer wanting to show them off. And it's true that there is something compelling about new friends, although that doesn't always mean we want to share them. Sometimes we want to keep them to ourselves, unwilling to sully them by exposure to our older gang or risk them being taken over by someone else. Introducing new people into an existing friendship group can ruin that energizing quality they brought when they were yours alone.

New friends can emphasize the way we are frequently different people with different friends. Occasionally there is a meeting where these disparate sides of us are in the same room at the same time and it can be hard to decide which one should dominate. Which person do you want to expose to someone who has never seen that side of your character before?

Within my own friendship wardrobe, there are some, although sadly few, men. I envy women who have gay best friends who are on hand for a deep dive into wardrobe concerns and have comforted them over the years when their romantic lives were rocky. They add a different element to the friendship wardrobe.

Instead, many of my male friends are those with whom I might have had a different kind of relationship had the fates not taken us in other directions. We have regular but not frequent lunches where usually more wine than is entirely advisable is drunk and I sway into the street convinced that the world is a better place than when I arrived. These men are more jocular and light than my female friends and any time the conversation gets a bit deep, they will manage to skew it away from being too emotional.

Unlike with female friends, there is a degree of disassociation between us that is helpful. It is true that you can lose a male friend when he marries or commits to another person who doesn't much like either his old gang or individuals within it, but more generally, there is a tacit understanding that this friendship is ring-fenced. Ideally we would like each others' partners, but we try our best to leave a wide margin for error around that issue. And generally we see each other without them. With female friends, it is much harder to maintain that sort of distance. Their dislike or disapproval of a partner oozes out.

Friendship between men is such a different beast. No less intense but often focused on more abstract concerns than the personal preoccupations of women. I watch my son with his male friends who have been his companions in life for many years and see how much pleasure he gets from chatting and joking, playing poker, watching golf or placing bets on just about anything. But when something emotionally difficult occurs, he doesn't turn to them for immediate, on-the-ground support. And this is not a solitary case. When I was in hospital a couple of years back with a dangerous pulmonary embolism and David was by my intensive-care bed all day, he told me he returned home at night and couldn't think who he could call to talk to about what he was feeling, either men or women.

During difficulties, it is wonderful to be able to delve into that friendship wardrobe and find various people there to help. Often what is most wanted is to escape the problem, while at other times, you want someone to listen while you talk endlessly about it. Listen, mind you, not jump in offering solutions.

Not all our friends are able to make us feel what we want them to make us feel at any given time. Sometimes friends' reactions are unexpected. Those you predict will not understand or be sympathetic to a situation can be surprisingly soothing. Those expected to instantly cheer you up manage to say something that makes you feel far worse, which is even more upsetting if they are meant to be the solution. It's the same as clothes. You don't really know whether they are going to work until you try them on.

In Search of the Eighth Wave

The wave will be both high and wild.

Sometimes an idea comes along and resonates with some part of the psyche for no predictable reason. Just such a thing happened to me with the Eighth Wave.

We were having lunch on a beach in the Portuguese Algarve in the early autumn. The weather was still warm and the long stretch of sand, interspersed with small coves, was baking hot, but there was the usual blustery wind of that coastline and the Atlantic water was cold.

I was staying in the region on a very desirable assignment to review Villa Joya, a hotel steeped in expensive understated luxury, particularly known for its elaborate and inventive menus. As an alternative to this, just below the main hotel was their beach shack serving drinks and lunch. There are many shacks where you can eat the local seafood and drink icy cold beers and the slightly fizzy *vinho verde* of the region on the beach, but there was nothing at all shack-like about this one's food or the service. Only the white-painted wooden structure qualified it as a shack. It was situated on a sheltered cove, set back from the waves which repeatedly crashed onto the rocks and the beach.

We tucked into the Japanese-inspired menu, watching the surfers who had gathered that lunchtime in the sea. Sometimes they would appear, dramatically riding the crest of a wave or crouching in the barrel as it broke, but frequently it looked as if they were just treading water and not doing much other than holding on to their boards. When I asked our South African waitress if she knew what was going on during this time, she said, 'They're waiting for the Eighth Wave' and before I could ask her to explain, she rushed off to serve another table.

What was this all-important Eighth Wave? I assumed it was something to do with attempting to harness the one likely to provide the most splendid ride. But watching the surfers, I couldn't tell if that was the case or not.

Later that afternoon, when I was attempting to swim a little further down the beach where the waves were tamer, I tried counting them in myself to see if there was anything special about the eighth one. I was too near the shore for this to really apply, as by the time they were near me, distinctions between them were minimal, but even so, looking at the waves coming in, I couldn't see or feel any difference between the seventh or sixth or even ninth wave and the eighth. All I could tell was that the first waves coming in after the largest were small, harmless things.

Determined to discover more, I did some basic research on surfing and learned various bits of terminology about the different types of waves and what kind of an experience they provide. I read about the importance of the contours of the ocean floor, with steep drops producing the 'plunging waves' that provide the excitement and the gentler slopes unsurprisingly delivering gentler 'spilling' waves. And I discovered that waves come in sets, which are clear to see even if you are just sitting on the beach, and that surfers do indeed count them in to help them catch the wave that will provide the blissful experience they are searching for.

But I didn't find out anything specific about my Eighth Wave. Undeterred, I asked a few of my surfer pals and still had no luck. With dogged determination, I refused to give up on the Eighth Wave, because the phrase had such appeal and I liked the idea of it being a metaphor for the ultimate experience. If that was what it was.

In my hunt for clarity, I came across various suggestions as to what this term might mean. My favourite came from John, whose father-in-law Richard is a surfer. Also, as it happens, like the waitress a South African. He told me it sounded a little like what Richard's surfing buddies call 'waiting for Leonard', a reference to a line in Leonard Cohen's 'The Stranger Song'. Cohen sings, 'Like any dealer he was watching for the card that is so high and wild, he'll never need to deal another.' Cohen never got things wrong.

Among those surfers, 'waiting for Leonard' describes the practice of paddling far out to where the biggest wave of the day will break. It will be both high and wild and, if they manage to catch it, that ride will make their day. Maybe their year. Sometimes, John continued, people speak of the seventh wave and 'waiting for the eighth' is probably just pushing your luck and hoping for an even better experience.

Someone else told me the expression came from *Papillon*, Henri Charrière's highly embellished autobiography which became a bestseller in the 1970s and was later made into a film starring Steve McQueen. Charrière – nicknamed Papillon – is wrongly convicted of murder and, after many years' imprisonment in various places, ends up incarcerated on Devil's Island, off the coast of French Guiana. The island is regarded as inescapable, but Papillon studies the waves below the cliffs and works out their pattern. One wave is regularly produced which is large and powerful enough to carry a floating object back out to sea.

He devises an escape plan which involves tossing sacks of coconuts into the water to use as a flotation device onto which he will be able to throw himself and literally float away in a dramatic escape. He pulls this miraculous feat off. That would have been an ideal explanation of the Eighth Wave. Except it turned out that Papillon's saviour was the seventh wave, not the eighth. Close, but no cigar.

Another moment when I thought I might have cracked it was when someone told me that the second side of the Kate Bush album *Hounds of Love* was called 'The Eighth Wave'. Perhaps that would provide an answer. But that title turned out to be 'The Ninth Wave', and anyway, didn't have any of the thrilling excitement I was attributing to my Eighth Wave; it was instead a very complex seven-track tale of being shipwrecked and alone and despairing in the water. Not the same thing at all.

A year later, I am still obsessed, despite almost all my research coming to little other than information on various different waves. Perhaps waiting for the Eighth Wave is really about waiting for the most desirable and thrilling thing that could happen, but which never does. Just waiting for the impossible. Never giving up hope. Perhaps I am waiting for the Eighth Wave.

Younger and More Modern

Most hair epiphanies happen because they promise a better life.

Why do we have good and bad hair days? All we can be sure of is that we have almost no control over how our hair will appear if left to itself on any given day and certainly none over how it grows. Yet the state of our hair is a huge determining factor in how we feel. It can be lank or bushy, tangled, dull or limp. It can make us feel sullen and despondent, hopeless, defeated. Or alternatively optimistic and generally pleased with how we are going to present ourselves to others and therefore how the day will go. Sometimes, actually frequently, hair is like a recalcitrant child who, no matter how much we coax and urge, refuses to do as we wish. We are left having to deal with the way it is behaving and make the best of it.

It's a curious fact that most of us wish our hair to be other than it is. From a very early age, we have an awareness of what it does and doesn't do. I remember the screams of my two-year-old niece when she couldn't keep her halo of strawberry-blonde curls straight, the way it was if she pulled it down hard when it was wet in the bath. My close friend, a naturally curly-haired woman, lives her life according to her hairdressing timetable, so her hair never appears anything other than in a condition of rigor mortis. Her movements are determined by the weather forecast and the avoidance of any rain which might make a dreaded curl appear.

Currently, my hair is unusually short. That is, it hangs in that no-man's-land between chin and shoulder. I generally feel more myself when it reaches the shoulder, but the other day, tired of the inches of summer-frazzled strands, I asked George, who cuts my hair, if we could do something different.

'What would you like?' he asked, standing behind me, pulling pieces away from my scalp to examine and, as I have said before and will no doubt continue saying for the rest of my life, I replied, 'I don't know. What do you think?' That's what *he* was meant to know. Hairdressers, like dentists and tennis coaches, are meant to know the correct form of treatment. They are meant to know what we should do. We want to have faith in them. No, it's more urgent than that. We *need* to have faith in them. If we can't trust *them* to conjure up a solution, then what's to be done?

We agreed that going shorter would be good, as would chopping into it here and there. George said we had to avoid the tricky issue of the jowl, which is the area his clients are most concerned about drawing attention to, tactfully omitting that he meant most of his older clients. I am sure his client Alexa Chung doesn't fret about jowls. Once my cut was finished, as often happens, the other stylists in the salon – generally very young and dressed in denim and elaborate sweats – gathered round to exclaim enthusiastically that it was great. That it was younger, more modern.

When you are over 50, younger and more modern becomes a requirement of a haircut in a way it never was previously. Before then, I went to the hairdresser for a variety of reasons, but not those. I couldn't imagine hearing those words when I stood up and shook the cut strands from the gown.

Most people's hair journey could be the basis of their autobiography. It's such a crucial ingredient in how we see ourselves, which is possibly why my hair frequently looks a bit of a mess to others, though not to me. I see it not as a mess, but as a demonstration of a certain relaxed attitude to appearance. Though of course some days I am less relaxed about it than others.

When I was editing *Vogue*, I was surprised to read a comment from my boss one day in the national press. He said, to paraphrase, that I was doing a great job but he wished I used a hairbrush more often. This was clearly a strange thing for an employer to say publicly and particularly so since I was in charge of a magazine whose USPs were style and knowing what was right when it came to appearances. But those words transported me straight back to the age of seven, when I joined a new primary school.

The classroom was up a flight of stairs and outside was a small landing with a piano, where every morning my mother would do battle with my hair and a brush. Arriving at a new school at that age, I didn't know anyone and, while the rest of the class had made friends and formed allegiances, I was mortified by my introduction to them being this humiliating activity taking place every morning. That tussle clearly informed my attitude to the hairbrush. It was an unpleasant instrument designed to turn me into something I wasn't. As cleanliness is meant to be next to godliness, so neat hair appears to designate some elevated state. One I have never personally subscribed to.

When I joined *Vogue* in my mid-thirties in 1992, I had long hair similar in style to mine as a teenager. In the intervening years, I had had a perm which I hoped would make me look like Maria Schneider in *Last Tango in Paris* and which, to be honest, didn't make a bad job of it. When that grew out, I had a not-very-successful very short crop with a fringe, but by the end of the '80s, it was long again.

Nicky Clarke, the celebrity hairdresser of the day, offered to take charge of my hair when I got the job of editor-in-chief. Free haircuts by the top hairdressers is one of the undoubted perks of those roles. I once calculated how much money it was saving me annually when it came down not only to cuts and colour, but also to the styling that needed to be done before events. It must have been around £20,000 a year – and would possibly have been more if I had been the kind of person who liked spending hours in the hairdresser's chair.

About nine months into the *Vogue* editorship, I was sitting in his Mayfair salon, a boudoir of gilt and velvets where Nicky, a high-voltage scissor-hands, would flash his shears in a theatrical manner, wearing leather jeans and Versace shirts, his own ginger hair a tumble of dried waves. I was, as usual, waiting for Nicky, who was always so late you thought he wasn't going to turn up at all, and by the time he arrived, I had persuaded myself that in the unlikely event he did appear, I wanted to return to the office with a radical crop. I was inspired by some of the waif models who were just starting to feature in the magazine – part of the short-lived but hugely influential grunge movement that was the stylistic hinge that turned the '80s, with their Chanel gilt buttons and ruffled cocktail dresses, into the '90s.

Despite the fact they were teenage girls and I was by that time a 35-year-old editor in charge of the most famous magazine in the country, an urchin cut struck me as some kind of solution – although, as with most haircuts, I had no idea what it was going to be a solution to. Most hair epiphanies happen because they promise a better life in some amorphous way.

Two hours later, I emerged with a Jean Seberg meets Isabella Rossellini crop. The next day, a newspaper ran a story about my new hairdo (an action which could only be regarded as the very epitome of a slow news day), but it did illustrate how people are fascinated by hairstyles. Volumes are read into how the Princess of Wales is wearing her hair at any given public event, or into Michelle Obama's braids and pieces, now that she is comfortable to play around with her hair, the White House years behind her.

A few weeks after that cut, a long interview with me ran

in *The Sunday Times*, alongside a beautiful black and white picture where an anonymous commentator was quoted as saying she was sorry I had cut my hair short. It was as if I was giving in. I suppose she meant that by losing my long hair, I was moving away from being the free-spirited woman she associated with that look to become more of a chilly, calculating executive. That I had been forced by some kind of collective to abandon my natural self and turn into a cliched template of a magazine editor. None of this was true, of course. I decided to get my hair cut radically short in a rather sad attempt to reach back to something youthful – the style of those models who were now floating around my pages in bias-cut slips and Converse trainers. It was that persona I was hankering for, not a transition to a formidable, *The Devil Wears Prada* editrix.

But back to younger and more modern. Youth and hair are inexorably intertwined. I remember, when I was much younger, an older man I was in love with commenting, with a kind of wonderment, on how soft and shiny my hair was. I also remember thinking this an odd observation, since I didn't think my hair was particularly either and no different to other people's. But now I am no longer young, of course I realize, yes, that it was soft and shiny comparative to what happens next.

Hair becomes brittle as we age. The follicles release less of the sebum that keeps it softer, and grey hairs don't retain moisture in the same way. I look now at the young Japanese girl seated opposite me on the Tube, her roots deliberately left a sleek Vantablack, before the rest is dyed a vivid cyclamen that reaches to her waist. It looks astonishing and I wonder if she knows how fortunate she is to have that spectacular young hair.

When I left my job at *Vogue*, I thought I might let my hair turn grey. It was something I had frequently considered, along with giving in to elasticated-waist trousers and spending afternoons making soup. Allowing my hair to turn grey now would be an expression of freedom and an admirable acceptance of time passing and being comfortable in what life brings us. Wouldn't it?

It would, of course, be liberating to stop the monthly visits to my colourist Melanie, during which we debate whether it's just a root job this time or if I need something a bit more. We discuss how perhaps the front should be a little lighter, and imagine how the colour might look after I've been in the sun. And it would be a relief to no longer have to look in the mirror and get involved in the monthly calculation as to exactly how many days longer I can go before the hints of silver that will have crept into my hairline go the whole badger.

But it hasn't turned out that way, and due to the attentions of Melanie and others over the years, my hair remains an approximation of the colour it always has been.

It's hard to analyse why I don't want to let my hair go grey; to give the simplest answer – that I feel I just look older – is lazy, since what does that actually mean? Other than we are a few steps nearer to death? There are many things that make us look older – the way we no longer walk quite as carelessly, our skin tone (both in terms of shade and texture), the way all of our torsos have thickened not just in width but in depth... I won't go on. But grey hair is such an immediate signifier of age (for most people) and generally doesn't look as flattering as other colours. We weren't born with grey hair. Letting it go grey is an acknowledgement that a part of us has given up clinging onto our younger selves. But keeping it coloured has also to be an acknowledgement of not wanting to accept the inevitable.

Nora Ephron, who, with her book *I Feel Bad About My Neck*, has become the patron saint of writing about ageing and appearance, even gives the credit for there being more older women in the workplace to hair colour: 'There's a reason why 40, 50, 60 don't look the way they used to, and it's not because of better living through exercise. It's because of hair dye.'

A year ago, David and I were staying at a small hotel on the Chatsworth estate in Derbyshire. As we ate lunch, I noticed that almost all the other guests in the restaurant were grey-haired couples; a hardy female group of hikers braving a table outside were also uniformly grey. But there was one group across from us – two couples who had made a late entrance. The young women were thickly made up with perfectly coloured dark brows, deep tans and hair as smooth as cellophane, one very blonde and one very brunette. The men were sockless, wearing patterned shirts and narrow cotton trousers. They were served champagne and brought a huge what looked like tea although it was only 2pm – silver tiers of sandwiches, some pork pies, scones and cakes, which the women immediately started to photograph. They were different to the rest of the diners. They were young.

I found myself uncertain where I fitted into this picture. I didn't associate myself with the many tables of grey-haired couples – the men in soft, comfy shoes and the women in waistless, forgiving dresses. To my eyes, they looked older than me and yet I should acknowledge that I was much closer to them than I was to that younger table, not in only years but probably in most aspects of life.

The rest of the afternoon, as we walked through the Chatsworth parkland, I pondered about this indeterminate state I regard myself as inhabiting. Not elderly. Heavens, no. But not, even with the most optimistic interpretation, young.

This makes me more determined than ever to keep up the hair dye. Which is the reason why I, along with many others, make such regular trips to our hair salons and get told to pop up on that chair and asked if we want something to drink and some magazines to look at. We have hideous hairdresser's gowns tied around our neck that look as if they are preparing us for the executioner's block. Despite so many advances in modern life, nobody seems to have managed to design anything other than this item of clothing that will disguise the allure of even the most beautiful women (and over the years, I've seen many having their hair done).

We consensually spend an hour or so confronting ourselves in the mirror, looking pretty ghastly and consoling ourselves that almost everybody else in the room, with a head full of silver foil and a dark brown or slimy white potion daubed all over their scalp, looks similarly frightful. And all this we suffer because, when it comes down to it, we are in pursuit of that elusive 'younger and more modern'. And where better than the hairdresser to attempt, even if fruitlessly, to reach out and grab it?

Eyeliner

Make-up, like children, is a topic that can unlock the most recalcitrant conversationalists.

A few years ago, I was invited to be part of a delegation visiting the Sharjah International Book Fair. Sharjah, the third largest city of the United Arab Emirates, is not nearly as well known as its neighbour, Dubai; indeed, I'd never heard of it before I got this invitation. But I discovered it is regarded as the cultural centre of the region, priding itself on its promotion of literacy and art. It is also, somewhat confusingly, one of the most conservative of the seven emirates: traditional Muslim dress is worn, alcohol is banned and there is no socializing between unmarried men and women.

In preparation for the trip, I went shopping for some dresses that might comply with the modest dress code. Fortunately, this was when the 'trad wife' style emerged, though it was then known as prairie style and the shops were filled with long-sleeved midi dresses with high necks. Since they made me look like Jo March's grandmother, and

I have never been a fan of *Little Women* in any form, even to comply with the local dress code, I couldn't face wearing one. Instead I found some vaguely oriental-print floor-length shift in H&M, which was perfect, and at home, I dug out a pair of white leggings and a scarlet tunic I had bought for a full-moon party in the Red Fort in Jodphur, which I also packed in case they might come in useful. They did not.

Arriving at Dubai's Al Maktoum International Airport, I was treated like a VIP and escorted to a lounge to be served thick sweet coffee and Turkish delight while my passport was taken from me to speed me through immigration. After a nerve-racking wait for its return, I was eventually shown to a huge black Tesla whose doors swung open like wings, and driven 28 miles along the broad highway that links the Emirati cities. It was night and there was nothing to see outside the window other than the red tail lights of the endless slow-moving stream of cars in front and illuminated signs in Arabic by the road. I arrived at my Sheraton hotel, checked in and then took the car about a mile further down the road, to where Sharjah becomes the neighbouring Ajman (where alcohol is allowed) to find my colleagues on the trip, drinking margaritas under the bright moon as they dangled their feet in the warm waters of the Persian Gulf.

Travelling is always disorientating, but the more so when you travel alone and into a totally different culture. When I woke the next morning, I was able to see for the first time that behind my luxury hotel, with its cascade of swimming pools, palm trees and sun loungers, there was nothing but mile upon mile of empty desert. In the next plot to the hotel, there were only huge earth movers, the sand and the highway.

That morning, I was taken to the Sharjah Ladies Club, an utterly surreal place, mummified in its silence. There was an empty beauty salon and an ice rink where three little girls in jeans were skating bareheaded, watched by their mothers, all shrouded in black abayas. There was a library with *Harry Potter* books (hugely popular there with both adults and children), a few Jeffrey Archers and, most incongruously, in the café a single copy of Martin Amis's *Money*. The club, I was told, was also a place where, watched over by a female lifeguard, women could wear a bikini and lie on the beach. But I didn't see a single woman doing that during my visit.

The whole place was so confoundingly different from anywhere I had ever been it was difficult to find areas of conversation to bond with the women in their long gowns and headscarves who were showing me around. Many of those I spoke to on the trip were entirely uncritical of living in a society I couldn't contemplate – tolerating, or even seemingly welcoming, the heavy presence of surveillance cameras and the recording of all voice apps. They claimed these made Sharjah a safe world where women could walk at five in the morning and not feel threatened. One even went so far as to say, without irony, 'I don't know what you would have to do to be raped here.'

No doubt in Sharjah there is the same violence against women as everywhere else, but this extraordinary observation was spoken aloud over tea with a group of sophisticated women I was interviewing in the massive Dubai Mall filled with recognizable Western brands. What a contrast to the UK, where many women increasingly feel unsafe walking the streets late at night but in most sectors of society are allowed to wear whatever they want, mix with whoever they want, say whatever they want. Two utterly disparate worlds.

And then there was eyeliner. One of the young women who was in charge of guiding me around was wearing the most gorgeous deep-purple eyeliner, circling her clear, dark brown eyes below their perfect brows. I imagined it was a local kohl, but when I admired it, she enthusiastically told me that it was by Marc Jacobs. I remarked that I could never apply eyeliner immaculately like her, and she immediately gave me a brief lesson which included the necessity of painting it just *above* the waterline, not *in* the waterline the way I usually do. I decided that I would get hold of that Marc Jacobs eyeliner as soon as possible.

The other women laughed at the way I described how my eyeliner always got smudged, and suddenly the whole morning took on a different tone. Make-up, like children, is a topic that can unlock the most recalcitrant conversationalists. There we were, cultural and sociological worlds apart but twinned by our interest in a purple eyeliner.

Eyeliner is the most common make-up product across the globe and has been for centuries. Its first known use was in Egypt, and from 3100 BC, it was found in China, Japan, Africa, India – often used by both sexes. It's possible to see eyes thickly outlined in the earliest paintings and sculptures of so many societies. And a fascinating fact: the word *alcohol* comes from *kohl*, both of them connected to antimony, a grey metallic element.

That woman in Sharjah is not the only person whose eyeliner I have envied. Truth be told, I have more recommendations for eyeliners than I do novels. I know that it isn't actually the brand of eyeliner that would make the difference, but being able to paint it on correctly; however, I persist in asking anyone whose eyeliner I admire what type they use.

I've heard more times than anybody should have heard anything that Victoria Beckham's Satin Kajals do the trick and won't find themselves anywhere on your face other than where you intend them to be. And I have tried again and again to make this work. I've bought the brown Cocoa Pavé, the bronze Smoky Quartz, the Navy Noir and naturally the plain black. And I've watched Victoria countless times online give her demonstrations of how to do her 'smoky eye', placing the dots between the lashes, the shadow of smudge below, the sharp line above (and always with the pencil sharpened). The fault clearly lies with me. People swear by these products.

For someone who has such trouble with this particular item of make-up, it might seem easier to give it a miss, but whereas some people have a lifelong determination to become fluent in Mandarin, or read the whole of Trollope, or possibly run the Athens marathon, I am obsessed with mastering eyeliner. I know that there is nothing intrinsically hard-wired into the particular shape of my eyes that means I can't wear it, because I've been lucky enough to have many make-up artists over the years paint mine perfectly, escaping any smudge action. So, in theory, it should be possible to acquire this skill.

Which is what drove me to the beauty department of Peter Jones in Sloane Square, once more attempting to crack this problem. Peter Jones because in 2022, when the Ukrainian war broke out, we took in Violetta and Andrii, a young couple from that country who lived with us for 18 months.

I met them from the Stansted Express, dragging their small suitcases, Violetta wearing a Harry Potter (Harry Potter again) T shirt. She was small and serious-looking, with her hair in a plait, and both of them were unsurprisingly extremely apprehensive as I drove them to our house, first through the buildings of the City and then into the more residential areas. They were throwing themselves into a world where they knew no one, had no jobs and had never travelled to before. Violetta could speak English, but Andrii had none. It must have been terrifying for them.

Fast-forward to 2025 and Violetta is now a brand ambassador for Dior beauty, looking after the Peter Jones concession. She started off at the Bobbi Brown counter at Selfridges and then graduated to the more upmarket

Dior brand. Sometimes she sends me pictures of outfits she is planning to wear to elegant Dior events where she now looks sophisticated and assured. So different from the person who arrived.

Today she is in black trousers and a black jacket cinched with a smart Dior belt, her once quiet mouse hair currently a shiny, smooth, dark brown. Her lips are painted a bright red and she has perfectly applied black eyeliner. I ask her to teach me how to use eyeliner and which one I should buy, explaining that I can never make eyeliner work; as I sit at the counter, we discuss whether my underlying skin tones will suit blue, which is what I want, and if so, what kind of blue – cobalt, pale, electric.

She teaches me that if I want the eyeliner to stay put, I need to first dab on a base of some pale eye shadow or foundation. Then, and this is an important piece of information, instead of just swiping along my eyelid, I have to drag my sagging skin up while looking down to allow me to paint the colour just at the lash line. I have to make sure the line is solid.

'If you don't fill the gaps it's going to look weird,' she tells me. 'There are a lot of things to talk about.'

'About what?' I ask, trying not to move my eyelid till the line is dry. 'You mean eyeliner?'

'Yes, like there are lot of techniques. Don't be afraid to use make-up remover to get it right. I feel like a lot of girls are nervous about make-up remover.'

She is explaining this while extending the line into a small flick at the corner of my eye. It is November 2025, and Trump and Putin are trying to carve up Ukraine. In recent days, there has been a volley of new attacks on Kyiv, so I think maybe Violetta is thinking there is lots to talk about what is happening back in her homeland. But as she always does, she bats away conversation about the turmoil there, where her mother still lives.

She shrugs. 'It's because there's a negotiation going on at the moment and that's what they do when we are negotiating. It's the game.'

She then turns her attention back to my eyeliner, which, by the time I leave, looks pretty good and has taken about 30 minutes to perfect.

I leave with a new khaki-coloured liquid liner and a lipstick that appears pale blue but actually paints your lips pale pink. Later that evening, Violetta sends me a text: 'Setting with powder on top may help, may not as well... I've never met a perfect pencil that will not smudge at all.'

On my way home, I spot a young woman on the Tube escalator. Staring into a small mirror with intense concentration as the escalator moves up, she adds to the pronounced cat-flick already there, with total precision and completely impervious to the rush-hour crowds. By the time the escalator reaches the top, she has perfected it, snapping the mirror closed and walking off into the night.

Alone

Being alone transforms the familiar space of home into something quite different, a little like one of Rachel Whiteread's artworks, where it is the empty space that is made solid rather than the external structure.

One spring morning, I had just settled myself on the battered old chair by the window in the bathroom with a cup of coffee and a copy of Alan Bennett's diaries, which are so relentlessly entertaining I read them on repeat. It was a moment of delicious pleasure which, even as I was experiencing it, I anticipated being disturbed by my then boyfriend David's arrival in the room, quite reasonably, to do his own toilette. As he appeared, I pondered the impossibility of achieving the ideal balance between all the advantages of living with somebody and enjoying their company and the undoubted appeal of time and space alone.

Much has been written by women about this subject – the allure of an escape from familial demands or even just having a space they could call their own. Virginia

Woolf's seminal lecture 'A Room of One's Own' explores the need for women to be allowed space, the same space accorded to men, if they are to be creative. But space to just be is also precious. Along with space just to be alone.

One of my favourite non-literary lines on this subject is from the Carly Simon song 'Alone'. It begins with the line 'My going has nothing to do with you, I'm just taking the time alone', and when I was thinking about leaving *Vogue*, these words jumped into my brain for weeks before I made the decision. This was just how I felt about abandoning the huge task of managing the magazine for so long and all the people that necessarily involved interacting with. It didn't mean I didn't enjoy working with them, just that I wanted to know what I would be without them. After so many years of working alongside people, what on earth would it be like to spend much of my time alone?

Another female singer-songwriter, Lucinda Williams, whose 'Side of the Road' is a favourite I chose for my *Desert Island Discs,* explores this feeling further. She describes wanting to know what being on her own would feel like, even the sensation of the air and the sun on her skin without anyone beside her, but also in the knowledge that ultimately there is someone nearby in the car at the side of the road. And the subject is on my mind as I write because

I am quite untypically living alone for a short time in the home I share with David, who is abroad.

This condition transforms the familiar territory of my home into something quite different, a little like one of Rachel Whiteread's artworks, where it is the empty space that is made solid rather than the external structure. In my house, the hallway and staircase echo with imaginary sounds and the disturbing knowledge that I will see no one step into them. The kitchen is littered with shelves and drawers of crockery and cutlery, and hung with large pans that remind me this is usually a place for many people; it's rare for there to be just a single person at the table. The bedroom feels foreign as I climb into bed and wonder whether to try to read, turn off the light or switch on the radio to have a comforting voice, as I adjust to the fact that I will be alone there throughout the night.

The only rooms which don't manifest change are the bathroom, perhaps, despite the opening paragraph of this piece, because time spent there is more usually solo. And the room designated as my office, where I am generally alone. Sitting at my desk, I don't hear the silence of the empty house that resonates in the other rooms. There is just the barking of the neighbour's dog and the familiar noise of the boiler firing up.

It's been years since I lived alone. The first time was in the first flat I bought, back in those days when a 27-year-old could get a mortgage to buy a flat in London. It was a small one-bedroom, on the ground floor of a converted house, but it had tall ceilings, a living room that looked over a garden and a minuscule separate kitchen. The bay window of the bedroom was in the front of the building and was about 10 feet from the busy 52 bus stop, where there was always a queue for the bus that rumbled past from Willesden through to Victoria Station. Although I had installed metal venetian blinds, it took me some months to realize that the position I had adjusted the slats to meant that, far from shielding the room from the street, anyone could look directly into the bedroom at night when the light was on, a view that was particularly good from the top floor of the bus. It was a disturbing thing to find out on my first foray of living alone.

This was especially true since, six years previously, I had suffered very severe panic attacks – the chief symptom of which was that I could not be alone. If left alone, I was utterly convinced that I would die. I couldn't breathe, and I was simply terrified almost all the time, from the moment I woke with stomach-churning panic to finally going to sleep to the sound of a cassette designed to calm.

I had to have someone, anyone, with me, like a small child, and it meant returning to my parents' home during the second year of my degree rather than continuing to live with my university friends. Nowadays there is a greater understanding of panic attacks than there was then, but when mine were diagnosed, it was the first time I had ever heard of that phrase.

Although I eventually learned much more about how to deal with these attacks, the decision to live alone was fraught and complex. I knew I had to balance the knowledge of how important it was to prove to myself I was able to do this against the continually lurking fear of fear, ready to overcome my rational thinking.

The state of being alone can be desirable and empowering if done out of choice, but less so if out of necessity, as so many discovered during the pandemic. In their book *The Lonely City*, writer Olivia Laing describes their own experience of that state: 'It feels like being hungry: like being hungry when everyone around you is readying for a feast. It feels shameful and alarming, and over time these feelings radiate outwards, making the lonely person increasingly isolated, increasingly estranged.'

Being alone does not by any means automatically induce loneliness: it is perfectly possible to be lonely when surrounded by people and far from alone. That can be the most penetrating kind of loneliness.

Until I shared a flat with Paul, whom I later married and have a son with, I continued to live alone. I spent those years entirely in my personal space. I had all the opportunities to be creative that Virginia Woolf urged on us – not that I took advantage of that, even though there was no one to disturb me.

The contents of the fridge were entirely my choice, although I do remember, after breaking up with one boyfriend, bursting into tears when I looked inside and realized there was no point any longer in keeping a jar of his favourite Hellman's mayonnaise. I was completely used to the notion of finding everything in precisely the same place it had been left, no matter how long or short my absence. I could play what music I liked, whenever I liked, at whatever volume I chose. The bookshelves were also mine alone, reflecting my interests and personal history and nobody else's. The cupboards and wall space didn't have to accommodate anyone else's belongings or taste in art.

During those years, I was working in an office with many other people, but most frequently I would go to sleep and wake alone. I didn't appreciate the singularity of these experiences at the time. I had forgotten what it felt like to live with others and I didn't know that one day it would seem so alien not to have anyone else around. Not to sense another person's presence at home.

Now, decades after that first experience of living alone, there have always been boyfriends and husbands, children, nannies, au pairs, lodgers to share the space. The possibility of a night alone, away from them, became, briefly, a welcome treat. During fashion shows, I would stay in luxurious hotels in Milan, Paris, New York and sometimes other cities. Checking into the immaculate and impersonal space of the hotel room, liberated from the domestic routine I had left behind and having only myself to consider in that room, was a delicious freedom.

Originally, I would stay in the same hotel as the rest of the *Vogue* staff, but as the years passed, I removed myself to another – and yes, more expensive – hotel. I wanted the space offered by not being part of the team, a team I could never really be a part of anyway because of the authoritative role I occupied. I favoured traditional spots like Le Lancaster in Paris, where the rooms were graciously furnished with table lamps and curtains rather than centrally controlled spots and blinds. Or The Lowell in uptown New York, where my room was large enough to hold meetings and where you could, although I never did, light a fire.

Ordering a croque monsieur from Le Lancaster room service to eat alone watching CNN was a total indulgence, while there is something about room service shared with another person that strikes me as less of a pleasure and more like dodging the decision to go out and experience something different.

Occasionally, also in Paris, I would return to the hotel if I had a gap in my evening schedule and change out of my fancy clothes to wander around the nearby streets and immerse myself in the sights of the city: the cheesy but splendid flashing lights of the Eiffel Tower, or the regular chess players in the Parc Monceau. I would eat alone, in one of the thousands of corner brasseries with their plastic-plaited seats and zinc-framed tables, attempting to read a book – always difficult while eating – drinking a glass of kir, and smoking a Pueblo cigarette that I couldn't find easily in London. I experienced the sensation of what Lucinda Williams was writing about – the Parisian air on my skin, lapping up the atmosphere, uncontaminated by company.

The rest of the time, I would be alone in terms of being without family and closest friends, but not alone: part of the caravan of fashion editors, buyers, photographers, agents, journalists and, more recently, influencers that moved seasonally along the same routes to the same destinations – showrooms, fashion shows, restaurants, parties. There would be generally enormous champagne-fuelled dinners and parties, where all the same faces from press and retail who had spent the day watching the shows with each other would be hosted in hotels or spaces commandeered for the night. In the main, we were acquaintances rather than friends. In Milan, designers such as the Missoni family, or the Versaces or Ferragamos, would sometimes open their homes up. These places – palaces, really – frequently so unprepossessing from the outside, would be accessed by a tall single door facing onto the street which, once opened, led to palatial apartments that could easily cater for a hundred guests or more. It was a privilege to be there, experiencing this world and being in the company of others, but in truth, I always found it a relief to return to my hotel room, alone.

Many of the players in the industry, particularly the image creators like designers, stylists, hair and make-up teams and photographers, would spend the majority of their working lives in this curious no-man's-land, travelling in a semi-nomadic band, yet alone, away from family, home being somewhere they rarely spent time.

When I first arrived at *Vogue* and had to approve the budget for a fashion shoot in Nepal, I couldn't believe how expensive it was – then around £1,000 a page. A large amount was spent on flying in members of the team, such as the photographer's preferred hair and make-up people, from wherever they might be in the world. Why couldn't we just use the most convenient – aka less expensive – person, I wondered? But the leading photographers *Vogue* was using at that point, such as Patrick Demarchelier or Peter Lindbergh, considered that unacceptable. If we wanted to use their talents, we would have to pay for the set-up to be the one they wanted. It was their team or no team.

Over time, I came to understand why these characters were so demanding about various conditions. Of course it is easier to work creatively with people you know and trust and share a shorthand with. But it was also, I realized, that being in the company of this familiar crew prevented them from feeling alone in a strange place. They were the transitory family. The same applied to the insistence on the same room in the same hotel or, as Mario Testino did, always travelling with his own pillow, for which we would have to book a separate seat on the Eurostar.

It's similar to the way famous people won't travel without an entourage of some kind to prevent them being seen, unattractively marooned solo somewhere, with no one talking to them. Or the female movie stars who always have a less attractive girlfriend or PR sitting behind them at fashion shows. These are human security blankets.

For many reasons, we are all likely to have to spend time alone. Other than taking holy orders or possibly joining a cult, there is not really an alternative. By the time you are in your mid-sixties, it is impossible to ignore the possibility and reality of those who make up your world dying, not as a remote concept but as something that might happen at any time. As one friend put it, 'The tent poles are all going.'

When we are children, and if we are fortunate, we are surrounded by others who provide and care for us. We then reject them, often temporarily, in a determination to mark our adulthood and manage life without them. But for most people, there is then a life lived with a new companion or family of one kind or another and we come to rely on that as a norm. We share space and decisions. We have someone to turn to in the night if we are fearful, make plans with for the future, or even just have a sense of their presence in our day. We become unused to being alone. The prospect of having to return to that state can be terrifying, as our days have become moulded by another's company. Without them, we struggle to find another shape.

Over the years, we are taught to read, to write, to speak languages, how to do yoga, how to cook and any number of other life skills, but given the likelihood of at some point being alone, perhaps learning how to embrace that state, rather than avoid it, would be the most useful knowledge of all.

The Wedding Dress

Looking at myself in the unforgiving light of the changing room, I started to reconsider the whole business. Even fleetingly the marriage itself.

It's unlikely that anybody in the history of weddings could have looked less attractive than I did on the day of my first marriage in 1994. Even my sister made no objection when I made that comment to her not long ago. No 'Don't be silly. You looked so sweet.' Or, possibly worse, 'It was so you.' Just a complicit silence.

There was an excuse. My then long-term boyfriend had proposed to me on a Monday and said he had booked the register office for the upcoming Thursday. Would I marry him? This now appears to be an impossible feat, as apparently wedding banns have to be posted 28 days in advance, but all I can say is that both he and I remember this as what happened.

It was an unconventional approach, but we had had an unconventional courtship and were living apart at that time. It was one of those make-or-break moments and, after thinking about it overnight, I made up my mind to accept and phoned him the next day, both frightened and elated to tell him my decision.

There was no time to organize anything, especially not something lovely to wear. In my experience, the more important the occasion you are trying to find something for, the less likely it is you will find it. That's why it's worth buying anything you fall for when you see it, and then waiting for the right time to come to you. As it invariably will.

Be that as it may, I didn't have anything appropriate for a marriage in the wardrobe and ran into the top London boutique Browns on South Molton Street, near my office, with my friend and colleague Frances. There wasn't anything that I really loved but, given the time shortage, I plumped for a long-sleeved white dress by the then fashionable Ghost and a richly embroidered Dries van Noten shawl in layers of silk and tulle.

Possibly because I had been miserable about having broken up and fearful about what my future would be, I wasn't looking my best at that point. Photographs of the day show me with a simply dreadful haircut that was intended to be a desirably messy shag but instead was just messy, a pasty pallor and an outfit that did me no favours

– draping me in shapeless fabric. Fortunately, my sister Nicky and her husband Con were the only witnesses, both of the marriage and my appearance.

It's one of my regrets in life that I looked that way on that day. Not hugely serious, but enough to remind me that if something doesn't feel right, it's better if need be to stick to something you feel good wearing. That dress never felt right. It was too sloppy and informal. The shawl made me look like the great-aunt of a Hindu bride.

Weddings have become big business, which is particularly surprising in the light of the high divorce rate, estimated in the UK as 42 per cent in 2025. Despite the stats, the amount of emotion and time and money invested in weddings is on the increase.

The whole business of getting married seems to become ever larger. Not only the wealthy and famous have turned it into a multi-layered event often lasting several days. No longer does a tent in the back garden and all over by teatime do the job for many. My stepdaughter managed to have a wedding and party in London and then another fabulous two-day party on the English south coast and still feel short-changed that she never managed to squeeze in a hen do – even though by this time, she and her husband already had a wonderful one-year-old daughter.

And the outfits are crucial to these celebrations. Brides have a whole wardrobe to stress about for the rehearsal dinners, the hen parties, the after-parties. In recent years, Sabine Getty's Schiaparelli gown involved 500,000 gold sequins, while Lauren Sánchez's bespoke Dolce & Gabbana wedding dress included 180 silk-chiffon-covered buttons.

Rarely is there an item of clothing so laden with emotion and hope as what, for these purposes, I am calling the wedding *dress*, though nowadays it may not be a dress at all. Although marriage is meant to be a joining of only two people, any fool knows that the wedding is a free-for-all, with opportunities for anyone and everyone who possibly can to get involved with recommendations and advice.

No wedding gowns, though, are freighted with such import as those of royal brides. Some weeks after the engagement between Prince William and Catherine Middleton was announced in 2010, I was contacted by a member of her team asking if I might come in and have a chat about potential designers for her to consider making her dress. Naturally, I was honoured, but extremely apprehensive. Wedding dresses are not, as I have pointed out, my strong point. And this gown had to encapsulate a nation's dreams and expectations.

From the moment the wedding was announced, the tom-toms began to beat about who would get the much-desired commission. This was no simple assignment. Catherine would need to work with a designer able to honour the tradition of royal wedding dresses, which come loaded with all the symbolism and heritage attached to that historical event. Every detail would be scrutinized and analysed for decades to come.

The gown was also needed to be the work of a British designer with the exceptional skill and imagination required for a job of this status, but also able to carry out the whole business in complete secrecy. Security was a big concern. It was essential that their identity didn't leak before the day.

They would also need the confidence to deal with the undoubted formality and regulations of the royal household while forging empathy with the bride-to-be. After all, she had to feel comfortable with the designer seeing her in all states of undress and possibly at different junctures in the process where she might be feeling unsure. My gut reaction told me a woman would be the best solution.

When we met, Catherine was keen to know my thoughts and we crouched on the floor of one of the reception rooms in Clarence House, looking at pages torn out of *Vogue*, showing British designers that she might consider – Erdem, Vivienne Westwood, Catherine Walker, Bruce Oldfield, Alexander McQueen, along with established wedding-dress designers like Phillipa Lepley. From Catherine's reaction to these, it was impossible to read what she thought.

At this stage, her usual wardrobe wasn't full of designer clothes and was similar to that of many young middle-class, middle-England women, featuring brands like Reiss and Jigsaw. She wasn't familiar with the process of custom-made clothes nor of working with a high-profile designer.

It was a different situation to that of the late Queen Elizabeth's wedding dress in 1947. That was designed by British couturier Norman Hartnell, a man the then princess already had a close relationship with, as he had worked on much of her wardrobe. In those days, there were no brands like Reiss or Jigsaw. The royal family's clothes were all made individually for them.

Hartnell's gown was embroidered with crystals and seed pearls depicting white York roses, and wheat sheaves to symbolize regeneration after the destruction of the recent war. Around the hem were garlands of orange blossom, often used in royal gowns to demonstrate fertility, chastity and virtue.

In her book *Fashioning the Crown*, Justine Picardie quotes Hartnell's memoirs, which tell how the precise origins of the material used in the gown were scrutinized. 'What was the nationality of the worms that had provided the silk from which the satin was made and from which I intended to make the dress?' he wrote. When it emerged that he was planning to use a satin from the Scottish firm of Winterthur, he was told that certain circles were trying to stop this on patriotic grounds – the silkworms involved might be Italian, who were not our friends in the war, or, possibly worse, Japanese. It's a sign of the way times change that when it was announced that the worms were fine – they were Chinese – Hartnell was given the all-clear to go ahead. Nowadays we might be far more wary of Chinese worms than of the Japanese versions.

Before I left that afternoon, Catherine asked me who I thought would be best. Although until that moment I hadn't had a firm favourite, I considered the options in front of us and suggested that Alexander McQueen – then designed by Sarah Burton, who had taken over the role of creative director after his death – would be a good choice. Sarah had a quietness about her that I thought would suit the bride-to-be, but also a strength of opinion and great expertise. Lee McQueen, as he was known, had long used symbolism in his work, and rich craftsmanship was a keynote of the house. Catherine just nodded and thanked me for all the help.

It was only when I was seated in Westminster Abbey on the day of the wedding and got a text through from my assistant Sacha announcing that the dress was indeed McQueen that I had any idea Sarah had landed the prestigious job. In the abbey, none of us could see what was happening outside and so missed the great reveal moment in real time. I am sure I was not the only person who made the recommendation, but I was very happy that final dress was not only perfect for this historical ceremony but also that the new princess forged a relationship with Sarah that would last for years to come.

Which brings me to my own second and relatively recent wedding. This time, I had slightly longer to find something to wear. David and I had been together for over 20 years, and had been talking for ages about getting married, or more frequently about not getting married. There was always another reason not to make the decision. But after my mother died, something shifted. It was impossible to push the powerful recognition of the passing of time to the back of my mind. There wasn't forever to keep batting this ball around. Tomorrow might not arrive. We needed to decide either to go for it or not. This time, we booked a slot in the Kensington and Chelsea register office (the same site as my first marriage) six weeks in advance.

We had kept the news relatively private and planned a minuscule ceremony, but with the photographs of my past wedding running on a carousel through my memory, I knew I had to do better on the clothes front this time around.

But what is a suitable wedding outfit for a second wedding in your fifties or sixties or later? In general, the situation does not obviously lend itself to the big white wedding dress treatment – unless, see above, you are Lauren Sánchez Bezos. It's not age that is the issue, but how much you want to present as the traditional, virginal bride.

Weddings are a meaningful acknowledgement of a relationship between two people and while obviously there is no rule about how to dress for such a thing, I wanted my clothes to reflect how I felt about the marriage. In truth, at the time I was a little unsure what that was. Was it tempting fate to marry at such a late age? Would our previously relatively harmonious relationship survive the new ties? Would marriage make us feel safer and happier?

Or would we both feel a new restriction in our lives together? Would I feel a sense of resolution? I had no idea.

Nor did I have any idea what I wanted to wear, only what I didn't want to wear. I was clear that I would avoid the type of floppy, swampy dress that David particularly hates and I rather love – the ones he calls my Demis Roussos look went on my no-go list. I wanted to buy something that I could wear again and ideally not only for very formal occasions. The wedding would be in late April, when the weather could go any which way, adding the usual British uncertainty to what was going to work. I didn't want to freeze on the steps of the register office, but neither did I want to be wearing a heavy coat. That, for some reason, didn't seem joyful enough. All white, I knew, was not flattering for me, and would also make me feel a bit silly. Navy – often my go-to – would be a little uncelebratory. Pink, perhaps, or green might be possible.

Surprisingly for someone who has had a long career running a magazine filled with suggestions of what to wear for what, I was paralysed with indecision. I didn't even know where to start. The thought of ordering endless items online and then having to organize boxes of clothes to be returned, each piece of clothing another failure, was too grim to contemplate. I knew I had to go to a real bricks-and-mortar shop to try the outfit on there and then.

So, as we all do in that situation, I went to a shop where I have often had success finding clothes – The Cross, a small boutique tucked into a corner of Notting Hill. But as soon as I arrived in the familiar colourful surrounds, hung with pretty, slightly boho-ish collections, I realized this was not the solution. The boho in me had long gone into retirement for something as formal as a wedding.

There was a brief moment when I thought the problem was solved by a cream linen coat embroidered with flowers and, on the back, a big yucca plant (yes, a smidge hippy). But I decided against it, and anyway a coat only deals with the outside and doesn't resolve what to wear beneath.

Eventually, only a week before the wedding, I took myself off to Liberty's, a department store with the great advantage of being a manageable size to navigate. I wandered around the floors picking up bits and pieces to try, knowing they were unlikely to be what I needed. Soon pooling on the floor in the changing room were the many midi and maxi dresses I tried on. Sleeveless floral numbers more suitable to a summer garden party, slithery bias-cut styles that didn't suit me, exotically printed columns that reached the floor, ditto.

Looking at myself in the unforgiving light, I started

to reconsider the whole business. Even fleetingly the marriage itself. Perhaps it would be best to stick to my edict of 'Wear something you are sure you feel comfortable in.' After all, it wasn't as if I didn't have countless dresses in my wardrobe from my years at *Vogue*.

Even so, that struck me as defeatist. Surely this marriage deserved better. The hunt would have to continue. Strolling mournfully towards the exit, I told the helpful sales assistant that unfortunately nothing worked – and then I spotted something perfect, coming to the rescue like the sight of land when lost at sea.

On the Jil Sander rail lined with otherwise monochrome tops and trousers, there hung a single pale pink satin pencil skirt decorated with small crimson poppies. I knew at a glance that it would fit me and was just what I wanted. And it was. The assistant, excited at making a sale but also caught up in the emotion of helping to find a wedding outfit, scurried around to find a suitable top. She returned carrying a fine-knit bright tomato-red cardigan by Dries van Noten and, the icing on the proverbial cake, a crazy red feathered bag by the same designer. The pencil skirt gave me a neat waist and hit exactly the right length below the knee. The cardigan was a flattering shape and the bag just the thing to make the outfit shout happily. Nothing swampy about it at all. I knew that I would wear that skirt again and again, and each time it would remind me of the day, but it would go on to have new memories attached to it.

And I delighted in going into my new married life as a scarlet woman, not a blushing bride. When you know, you know. And I knew...

Roast Chicken

A roast chicken is never simply a roast chicken.

Take one chicken, smear with butter (olive oil is fine if you are someone who worries about their butter intake) and rub with salt and pepper. Stuff half a lemon into the cavity and add a few whole garlic cloves in the roasting pan alongside the bird. Put in a medium-hot oven for an hour or so. I know some people turn the heat up high for the first 15 minutes, but I never bother and it doesn't seem to make much difference. Baste it once or twice if you remember and check it's cooked through. That's it.

The roasted garlic will emerge as crispy little nuggets with a soft core inside their skins and I frequently add in some small potatoes. These are not as good as proper roast potatoes which have been par-boiled and tossed in a little flour, but they are not at all bad and absolutely no trouble. This is the most basic way to roast a chicken and it's what I do usually once a week. It has never failed me.

A roast chicken is never simply a roast chicken. It's a food for making things right. In Simon Hopkinson and

Lindsey Bareham's cookbook *Roast Chicken and Other Stories*, Hopkinson writes that that title was chosen 'simply because it had a friendly ring to it'. He's correct. There is nothing adversarial about roast chicken.

I've never lived anywhere I considered home that didn't include roast chicken, although I can't recall eating it as a small child. I don't remember if the dish was on the menu when I was very young, since roast chicken makes most sense if there are number of people to share it and my siblings and I didn't eat with our parents until later. You don't roast a chicken for three children under six.

It would have been when my mother began to rent a house in the country as a way to get us out of our crowded London flat in the school holidays that she started to cook for us. And along with spaghetti bolognese and beef casseroles, her repertoire included roast chicken. Hers was always one of the very best. The way I cook mine is just like hers, although she would stuff the cavity with tarragon rather than lemon. Sometimes, as she did, I put some chipolata sausages in the pan as well.

She cooked it as frequently as I do and I wish I could ask her why, but that is one of the many questions that will never be answered now, after her death. I wonder if she found the same qualities invested in it as I do, in particularly a deep-rooted sense of home. But I suspect not. My relationship with this meal is probably founded on her providing it throughout our shared life, while her mother would never have cooked roast chicken. In fact, I doubt her mother cooked at all. My maternal grandmother's cooking was never once mentioned to any of us, and making a cosy home, our mother implied, was not one of her strengths. But again, it's too late now to discover.

The fact that I always cook the same roast chicken doesn't stop me poring over alternatives. There's a version by the American cook Alison Roman involving caramelized lemon and dates in a large casserole, which is delicious, but not what I consider roast chicken. One of the UK's best restaurateurs, Sally Clarke, has a recipe in *First Put on Your Apron* that suggests laying the bird on top of white onions, carrots and celery and turning it upside down for the last 25 minutes of cooking. A cookbook I remember from childhood is Arabella Boxer's *First Slice Your Cookbook,* cleverly designed to deliver the three different courses in different-coloured slices. She recommends using rosemary rather than tarragon and wrapping the bird in foil for the first 20 minutes. *The Constance Spry Cookery Book* differentiates between the English and French method of roasting chicken, the first involving stuffing and dripping, the second more like my own. Incidentally, here's a small but entertaining snippet. In the introduction to this vast collection published in 1956, Queen Camilla's father, Major Bruce Shand, is thanked not for his roast chicken recipes but for his contributions to the chapter 'Wines – their choice and serving'.

Some of the pleasure of roast chicken is how the dish makes no demand on the cook. It requires next to no preparation and causes no concern during cooking. But far more important is that the ease of roasting a chicken provides uncomplicated comfort. Roasting pork, lamb and beef are all more stressful and require a great degree of accuracy. The amount of effort involved with a chicken is minuscule compared to the pleasure the relatively bland-tasting bird gives. And because it is bland, it can be used as a reliable base to build upon, if that's what you wish. Stuffings, elaborate vegetables, white sauce or indeed any number of sauces can be added into this dish. But I never do.

I turn to it to relieve stress and anxiety. I cook it to welcome someone home or serve as a last meal before either they or I depart. When friends come over for supper, there is an odds-on chance that it will be roast chicken they will be served. I cook it because not only I – who would have it as my death-row dinner – like it, but so do most people. Even my son, who was an infuriatingly fussy eater as a child, has always enjoyed it. David likes a roast chicken, while he looks distressed when I serve one of the many terrific chicken-thigh recipes from Diana Henry's cookery books.

We're a breast-fancying household but, after using the leftovers to make stock, I strip all the meat off the carcass and eat it up in various rice dishes or cold lunch. Both the activity of making stock and using the leftovers make me feel as if I am efficient and thrifty in a way I really am not. It's typical of roast chicken to be endlessly helpful.

When I was editing *Vogue*, roasting a chicken was a quick-fire way to shed the skin of that role and the office day. I may have had to explain to a vital photographer why I didn't want to use his particular edit of photographs. I may have had to argue with my boss that our overspend on the magazine was entirely justified, pointing out how much money we made – over £12 million a year during the good times. I would often have to placate important advertisers who felt they weren't represented in the way they wished in the magazine – not enough pages. I may have been preparing for three weeks of fashion-show travel ahead and worrying about leaving my son behind with only a teenage mother's help. But when I was sitting at the table with him and the chicken and my stepdaughter Emma, the turmoil was calmed. Briefly, all seemed right.

Now that I no longer have that kind of a life, roasting chicken is still as important. It roots me when at times it feels as if I can't find solid ground beneath my feet. In some inexplicable way, it confirms me as a person I recognize. I still turn to roast chicken as a kind of reassurance. How wonderful it is to find in something so simple such a reliable panacea.

Lingerie or Underwear

Sensuous underwear is famously worn by women whose jobs require an almost sexless appearance.

There are very few women I know – actually, not a single person comes to mind – who refer to their bras and knickers as lingerie. The word, derived from the French for linen, *linge,* originally applied to a range of garments (another word no one uses in real life) in the late 19th century and refers to lightweight satin, silk and lace underwear rather than, for example, the sturdy Chilprufe vests some of us were put in as children or the five-pack white cotton knickers from M&S that many of us will have bought.

One early evening, I was walking along Piccadilly. There was a full moon above the sumptuous façade of Fortnum & Mason, its aura throwing a lunar halo as it hung over the chimneys. Standing on the corner of the street just by the Royal Academy of Arts was a man in a camel overcoat, of the kind worn by men who spend much of their life in that area of London, with its expensive restaurants, art galleries, gentlemen's clubs and financial offices. This man walked purposefully towards the bus stop with a straight military stance. He was clean-shaven with the disciplined hairline of a recent trip to a barber – old-fashioned, smart barber shops being another stalwart of this neighbourhood. From one hand dangled a small black carrier bag with the words Rigby & Peller, the store that owes its fame in great part to having been the corsetière to the late Queen Elizabeth. And earned a degree of notoriety as it was stripped of its royal warrant when the then owner published a book detailing information about its famous client.

There was something incongruous and delightful about this man standing there with this small bag. Did it contain something in red satin, skimpy knickers, a bustier or a tasteful cream satin bra? Was he taking this home to a wife, or visiting a lover, his wife safely at home or walking the dogs in Hampshire? Or perhaps he was buying it for himself? We will never know.

Underwear is frequently considered a sexually alluring tool, but in my own experience, for most of my life, I have found that my partners (male) appear distinctly uninterested in my underwear in any way other than to remove it as speedily as possible. I remember once making an effort to wear stockings and a suspender belt, which I imagined might have been appreciated by my then lover, but he didn't appear to even notice this unusual state of affairs.

The lack of interest in underpinnings may have been because many of my boyfriends came from a generation a little older than me; many of their girlfriends were focusing on ridding themselves of the trammels of bras, fingertip-control corsets and suspender belts, and so frequently wore none at all or nothing particularly interesting.

But elaborate underwear having been consigned to the category of objects that benefited men rather than women, the whole lingerie business bounced back again in the 1980s. Those bras and matching lacy knicker sets were no longer considered restricting markers of a women trapped in the male gaze, but had become emblems of female empowerment. These items which had previously been thought of as private, intimate equipment were now flaunted both as a fashion trend – Madonna in her cone-shaped Gaultier bra – and as the kind of treat a woman might indulge herself with. As women's work life began to mirror that of men, and our clothes did the same, so did the desire to separate ourselves underneath.

Delicious underwear that would certainly qualify as lingerie was a whole new big business. There was the hugely successful and borderline exploitative Victoria's Secret, with their cheap erotic knickers and fashion shows where their Angels strutted the catwalk in the stuff of pornography. Or that would have been the case back in the day, when porn included underwear. There was also the mass of new shops like Agent Provocateur and Coco de Mer, who were able to sell knickers and bras and suspenders as fashion women bought for themselves.

Beautiful sensuous underwear is also famously worn by women whose jobs require an almost sexless appearance. Sadly, I have no stats on how many in the regulation uniform of a Sainsbury's cashier or driver on the Bakerloo line wear, underneath their utility everyday clothes, purple lace bras and satin knickers, but if I were asked to lay a bet, I would guess a fair few. Ditto women required to do their jobs in a primarily male environment, from investment banks to foreign correspondents such as the late Marie Colvin, the famous *Sunday Times* journalist and also one of my close friends.

There was no war zone that did not exert a magnetic pull on Marie – Eritrea, Lebanon, Libya, Chechnya, Sri Lanka, East Timor, Iraq and her final journey in 2012 to Syria. She was driven by the frequently quoted journalistic mission 'to tell truth to power', to ensure the world knew about the brutalities happening in places the rest of us were safely insulated from, and by the hope that shining a light on what she discovered might result in change. But also by some personal and ultimately fatal drive that meant that she would always be the first one in and the last one out. The final story she filed on any trip was never enough.

But Marie was also a great girlfriend. She loved cooking and sailing, gossiping and hosting rambunctious parties and also shopping for clothes that she wore with elegance on her slim, athletic figure – including excellent underwear.

In fellow foreign correspondent Lindsey Hilsum's biography of Marie, *In Extremis,* she writes of Marie's time in East Timor: 'After her La Perla underwear was looted, she had claimed replacement costs on expenses. The (male) accountants rejected her claim on the grounds that underwear couldn't possibly cost so much. Her (female) foreign desk manager replied, "Marie's does."'

Then, a few months later: 'After seeing pictures of her in hospital in Sri Lanka [where she was wounded by a government grenade, ultimately losing an eye], an editor asked her to write an article about her "lucky red bra".

Marie pointed out "it was red only because it was drenched in her blood".'

Her taste in underwear became a part of the Marie legend. In 2012, she was cruelly targeted and blown up by a bomb in the Syrian city of Homs, where she was reporting, despite being urged by many not to go, on Bashar-al-Assad's brutal regime.

I would hate Marie's bravery, love of life and people, and incandescent energy to be reduced to the shorthand of what underwear she chose, but it does illustrate so much about her as a person: her delight in the sensual enjoyments in life – the sea, good food, expensive china and bed linen, along with the adrenaline of danger and her continual willingness to put the body that she loved to dress well in mortal danger.

Most of our attitudes to underwear do not carry such stories along with them, but even so, what we choose to wear reflects how we feel about ourselves.

It was only in the late 1990s that my own attitude to underwear changed. For most of my life, I had absolutely no nice underwear. The only remotely racy piece in the drawer was a pair of skimpy red lace knickers that a male journalist friend gave me for a birthday, much to the raucous pleasure of those around him, but I never wore them. Another gift, though, this one from my sister, of a satin slip by the designer Carine Gilson, had greater impact. Wearing this dark green, lace-trimmed piece immediately transformed me into – well, at one level, the kind of person who would wear such a thing, but on another, someone who was able to take pleasure in the sight of herself wearing it. Gilson's boutique was on the left bank of Paris alongside a series of other lingerie stores like Sabbia Rose and Princesse Tam Tam, and during the shows was a regular stop-off for the wealthier journalists and models like Naomi Campbell. Buying expensive underwear at home in London was something I would never indulge in, but in many ways, the shows were time out of time, with a what-goes-on-tour-stays-on-tour mentality, and silk slips could literally slip under the wire.

And then I met my current partner David, who surprised me by paying attention to what I wore under my clothes. He's not an underwear freak insisting I am bound up in silk and lace, but he will appreciate a pretty bra and is more likely to notice new knickers than he is a new sweater. As always when relationships are in their first blush, I was keen to cater for this and saw it as an opportunity to allow myself to buy lots of bits and pieces that would definitely qualify as lingerie, not run-of-the-mill underwear. But as the years have passed, like so many of the ways we try to please new partners, my dedication to this has faded.

Recently, I wrote an article about knickers for the *Daily Mail*. I counted that I owned 52 pairs, of which several were more than ten years old. This contrasted with the average British woman who some random but nonetheless compelling survey discovered owned 20 pairs – still a remarkably high number. A few in my drawer are scraps of colourful lace, many more utility cotton briefs. And several somewhere in the middle, I guess. I still sometimes wonder if I would ever actually speak of them as my lingerie.

The Dishes

I don't want to let you down,
I just need to get my feet up off the ground.
But there's still the dishes to do.

From 'The Dishes' by Christina Kulukundis and David Ogilvy

The ruins of Mystras, the once splendid centre of Byzantine power, lie north of the Mani peninsula, one of the three prongs of the Peloponnese which stretch down to the southernmost tip of mainland Greece. Mystras was built on the slopes of Mount Taygetos, above the plain of Sparta, now an unprepossessing modern town but once one of the most important cities in Greece.

I visited at the end of the 1980s for a short holiday with Christopher, an architect and Greek-history enthusiast who was keen to show off his considerable knowledge of the Mani, an area he had visited often. He had planned a road trip staying in cheap village hostels in the tiny villages along the coast, eventually reaching Cape Tainaro, thought in Greek mythology to house the entrance to the underworld.

I was heartbroken at this point and this expedition was intended, at least by me, as a distraction from my misery. We drove to Mystras straight from the airport and as we wandered through the ruins surrounded by cypress and pine trees Christopher attempted to conjure up the life of the city as it would have been, with its fortress, palaces and churches that could be just about imagined among the remains of homes and pathways scented by oregano, gorse and thyme.

But he had a hopeless audience in me. I was unable to engage with the stories he wove – of the many centuries of battles and transfers of power, of the once splendid architecture and the town planning. Instead I suddenly stopped short under one of the cypress trees and told him what was on my mind: I hoped I had remembered to bring the clothes pegs with me to go with my portable washing line.

One of Joan Didion's most quoted sentences is 'We tell ourselves stories in order to live.' Those of us who have read 'The White Album' essay it came from, one of her very best, will know this is the beginning of an exploration both into her disintegrating mental health at that time and the disintegrating health of Los Angeleno society in the late 1960s.

I have no such broad statement to make about living in the febrile, chaotic and, in too many ways, damaged days of 2026, when I state that I write to discover what I think, rather than to record what I already know. So it was that when writing of my philistine reaction to the wonders of Mystras, it occurred to me that there could be a childhood root to my preoccupation with practical domesticity. Thoughts of household chores constantly rumble below the surface, no matter how much more interesting a play, conversation or artwork might be. That particular to-do list is always predominant in my mind. Which I suspect is true of many women, but by no means all, and in my case bears no relation to the limited amount of time I actually engage with such activities.

Fast-forward 40 years and I am on another Greek holiday, this time with David. I went for a swim one late afternoon after we had made love and thought, as I moved slowly through the water, how, although I tried very hard not to let images of different cardboard packing cases clog up my mind, it was unfortunate that just a few minutes before we'd had sex, I had been looking up storage cases on Amazon and I couldn't get them out of my head. It was nothing to do with David or how I felt about him. Just the wretched way things like cardboard boxes can so often get in the way of things.

The stuff of domesticity has always taken up a large part of my mental capacity. As a small child, I would sit on the toilet with the seat down and watch our nanny do the washing. In this small bathroom I would watch her scrub our clothes in white Lux soap flakes, put them in the spin dryer to get rid of the bulk of the water and then hang them on the wooden pulley that hung above the bath. One of my most treasured toys was a small washing machine with its own mangle that I could wind wet pieces of cloth through.

It's not that my childhood home contained a splendid array of neatly organized storage of the kind we nowadays salivate over: ranks of glass jars stuffed with pasta and rice, decorative cans of chickpeas and flageolets and prettily wrapped tins of anchovies and sardines, or displays of collections of china and glass. There was none of that. The kitchen was small and entirely utilitarian rather than any kind of a style statement. There was a Formica-topped table where we children would eat our meals, but hardly any cupboard space for food. Two wooden shelves under the sink housed onions and potatoes and a small fridge the butter and milk and cheese, but most food was bought daily from the shopping street round the corner.

The shops were like the old-fashioned card game of

Happy Families: Mr Wood the Butcher, Mr Bainborough the Greengrocer, Mr Charles the Fishmonger, Mr Stokes the Stationer. Mr Wood would deliver meat which Gina, our Portuguese daily, would then mince in a metal mincer clamped to the table. The onion seller on his bicycle hung with onions and garlic would regularly ring the doorbell with his wares. The knife grinder and cane-chair restorer would also make regular appearances.

The thrum of domestic routine was soothing in its predictability and utterly recognizable as the world that was home. It made me feel safe, and perhaps such activity still does.

Our mother, though, was never part of this domestic scene. She would leave the flat in the morning to go to her office and until we went to school we children were in the care first of Janette, and then any other number of nannies and mother's helps, some like Janette wonderfully caring, others less so. This must have confirmed in my mind early on that it was not so much a maternal role, taking care of the home, but that it was all done by women. The household was a female zone. Our father engaged in zero domestic activity to a degree that would be unthinkable nowadays. He couldn't make a piece of toast or boil an egg. He never made a bed or washed up a glass. And despite working flat out, our mother considered this behaviour entirely normal. She once wrote, 'The accepted view was that domesticity was a woman's role and a man should be able to get on with his life.' No wonder I was steeped in the notion that this kind of thing was women's business.

Three decades later, I became a magazine editor working in an office just like my mother's, staffed primarily by women, many with children. I never felt I attained the ordered, streamlined domesticity of my childhood and, as many a working mother will know, life was endless firefighting. But although to me as a child everything appeared orderly, that was probably far from how my mother felt about her life. Childcare for both her and me was a constant anxiety. For those of us who had no family help and were paying for alternatives, the search for the right person to take care of our children was an endless preoccupation.

At one point in my diary at that time, as one of the many kind Australian or South African girls who looked after my son was about to leave, and I was soon to head off for a month of travel to fashion shows, I wrote desperately:

> I've only seen one possibility and the weeks are passing. Like houses and lovers, you only need to find

> that one at any given time, but the whole business means that they might well get another job while you are making up your mind. There are so many of us trying to find a nanny in the office that the fax is permanently occupied by the agencies – sending their terms and conditions, not CVs.

When I was not at home, these young women were the engine of my son's world – cooking for him, washing, shopping, driving, organizing his social life – and I wanted him to have that same sense of order and security that I had felt as a child. These women enabled me to do my job and, as in my childhood home, made our home life work. The entirety of my domestic to-do list was delegated to them and to the cleaner who came in twice a week. I might have thought about the housekeeping a great deal, but I wasn't doing any of it myself.

Nowadays I have as much time to be immersed in domesticity as I could wish for. Years of working in an office have given way to a checkerboard of different activities with gaps in the day when I could polish, tidy, decant and arrange as much as I chose. But do I?

When I left my job, I thought that I would be able to find pleasure in these activities. In making the house look perfect. My clothes would hang in colour coordinated cupboards and the books would have their alphabetically catalogued places on shelves rather than being crammed in randomly and stacked in piles wherever there was space. I would, yes, achieve that storage-jar paradise where I would never have half-used packets of pasta rammed chaotically into a cupboard, never quite enough in each for a meal and never quite sufficient rigatoni, fusilli or penne rigate of the same brand to add in to make the quantity needed.

In this new world, I would not start the day wearing nasty plastic garden shoes and apron, stuffing the leaves into the recycling bin when they have piled up so high and thick outside the front door that they are nearly impossible to wade through, as I once did before joining an immaculate Ralph Lauren for a breakfast at Claridge's. Nor, having crashed into a vast spider's web, would I head off to a similar meeting with the silver threads stuck in my hair, unnoticed till hours later.

Yet now that I'm so much more rooted in home, it isn't, as with so many imagined states, quite the way I thought it would be. The soothing quality of domesticity when somebody else is doing most of the work was something I hadn't quite acknowledged either – unsurprisingly as a child, rather less intelligently as an adult.

Nor had I appreciated the relentless, Sisyphean quality of domestic activity. Yes, I am able in the summer to hang out clothes on our washing line, something I have always enjoyed, but I now realize that it is the thought of doing this rather than the actual pegging out that I appreciate. I have no more interest in organizing a store or laundry cupboard than I ever did, because once this is done there is only a short time before the salt ends up with the cereal and the vinegar has found its way onto the biscuit shelf. Yes, there is time to turn the stock into a series of soups, but there is no lasting satisfaction in this. Ultimately, they just get eaten.

And yet, despite the transitory nature of domestic activities, there is still the sense of order they give. 'Dirt is matter out of place,' anthropologist Mary Douglas wrote in *Purity and Danger*, her book about cross-cultural classification and taboo. It is one of the very few facts I remember from my degree course and applies to so many areas. She was using it in explanation of the classification systems of different cultures – what qualifies as dirt when and to whom? But the underlying principle remains in all our homes. We don't want to see our olive oil, no matter how delicious and expensive, in the bathroom sink. We like our peat-free soil to be in the garden, not on the carpet.

Domestic tasks. They may not involve big thoughts and blue-sky thinking, but they are essential in keeping chaos at bay. No matter what else is going on – heartbreak, death, birth, elation – there are always the dishes to do.

The Myth of Effortless Chic

The women who we consider possess this desirable style...know what it takes to look that good and don't pretend otherwise.

The obvious statement that there is no such thing as effortless chic doesn't stop those two words being one of the most prevailing fashion slogans of our time.

The idea that a great result can be attained without having to exert oneself in any way is certainly compelling. If bottled, it would have as much value, possibly more, than gold. But not only can it not be bottled, it doesn't exist. It's a mirage – one of those sights so alluring from a distance, shimmering appealingly and for moments appearing real, that disappear entirely once you reach them. And when or if you drill down, all that is left is somebody wearing a pair of unremarkable jeans and an equally unremarkable white shirt.

Our school had a prize for trying hard that was awarded at speech day. It wasn't the prize parents most wanted for their child, but it was an acknowledgement that there was a worth in trying, even if it was fairly low down the ranking of achievement. Each time I see those two words, 'effortless chic', I want to remind whoever wrote them of this fact.

I blame this myth on the internet. Our digital universe has made short, simple concepts that don't take many words powerful tools for driving sales. Our click-through world no longer has the mental bandwidth to put up with lengthy expositions of why a certain pairing of a sweater and jeans is chic and another is just dull. Fashion writing has been distilled into easy-to-digest mantra, particularly in magazines and newspapers where editors need to drive online clicks.

The tragedy of effortless chic is not the appearance it conjures up, which is generally centred on a neutral range of colours – black, white, grey, navy – and simple, unfussy styling, more often than not accompanied by smooth, long hair. It's the soul-destroying idea that there is no value in effort, along with the convincing falsehood that chic is something you can follow a template for. No matter how many 'Ten Pieces for Effortless Chic' any of us might consider, we're playing a loser's game. There is no colour-by-numbers approach to looking like contemporary effortless role models like Gigi Hadid or Caroline de

Maigret – both of whom, I would suggest, actually spend quite a lot of time putting together their looks.

A Pinterest page I consulted on effortless chic came up with 670 pictures of slender, long-haired women dressed in jeans and a variety of vests and T shirts. It was hard to tell many of them apart. There was no individuality or experimentation. A confession here: in many of the pictures, I saw the very pair of brown-and-white-striped Adidas Gazelle trainers I own. And I can tell you for free that I frequently wear them and they don't look either effortless or chic, although it's possible that, when I bought them in Selfridges shoe department, I imagined for a moment they would contribute to that effect.

On that Pinterest page there was a disproportionate number of images of Jennifer Aniston over the years, generally exposing her admirably toned arms, and also Kate Moss, who is an excellent illustration of how chic is never effortless. I've never seen Kate looking less than chic, whether that be in black minidress at a funeral, transparent black shirt and bikini top on a Greek island, skimpy black dress and sheer black tights at a gallery opening or even in a pair of pyjamas cutting my son's hair in a garden in Chelsea. She is frequently held up as somebody who appears to have thrown her look together carelessly, with a perfect result. But, like most of the chicest women I have come across, she is not a quick dresser, nor does she have a pared-down wardrobe.

Her good taste is innate, but her look comes from a process of exploration and elimination that has been distilled into her style. Hollywood goddesses of the 1940s, Anita Pallenberg, Catherine Deneuve – all play their role in her wardrobe. There's nothing shaming about stealing from the best. But it's not effortless. Effortless denotes a kind of ignorance. That you just happened on it. Real chic like Kate Moss's is an art form. And, just for the record, includes fabulous, real jewellery.

In early 2026, *Love Story*, a TV series centred on the ill-fated story – and much-admired wardrobe – of the real-life Carolyn Bessette Kennedy and her husband John F Kennedy Jr was released on streaming platforms. Article after article described Bessette's style as effortlessly chic. And she certainly knew how to look wonderful, whether in a simple shift by her one-time employer Calvin Klein or a pair of Levi's, a black crew neck and flip-flops. She wore clothes that were accessible to all, including hairbands that held her thick blonde hair back from her face and white shirts with the necklines unbuttoned and cuffs turned up just so. As far as we, the public, could tell, she never looked undone or scruffy, although she never looked too done. The essence of effortless chic.

Except it wasn't exactly effortless, as was made clear by the extensive wardrobe team trying to source the exact same looks for the series. It involved work and the result couldn't convey anything like the same quality. That's because the chic is just as much a part of the individual's personality as the clothes. Although Sarah Pidgeon, the actress playing Bessette Kennedy, had the same rake-thin body, perfect blonde hair, East Coast pretty skin and some of the same publicity-shy mannerisms, she couldn't really ever have Carolyn's style, which of course was enhanced by association with the heady glamour so often preceding tragedy within the Kennedy clan.

The women who possess this enviable quality do not themselves tout the notion of effortless chic. They know what it takes to look that good and don't pretend otherwise. It's us who label them this way. Even though everybody knows there is no such thing as effortless chic, that doesn't prevent it being an idea that we almost wilfully subscribe to. Which is curious, if you think about it. How many notions that we know to be false still hold such compelling allure?

Type Two Fun

After all, when everything goes according to plan, there's no drama to be had in the retelling.

Type Two Fun was introduced to me by Michael VerMeulen, an exuberant Chicago-born journalist and friend. Michael was a gold-medal award winner in various kinds of fun, most of which involved copious amounts of substances and a high degree of wild and flamboyant behaviour.

Along with flaming red hair and pale freckled skin, Michael had a reportorial brilliance, an ability to spot great writers and an infallible nose for stories, hunting them out like truffles amid the thickets of the international papers he read every day. Unfortunately, this was twinned with an astounding absence of social intelligence and a variety of demons that ultimately led to his death in 1997, which the coroner recorded as a case of 'wild misadventure'.

His favourite stories and activities often qualified as Type Two Fun, an expression which applies to experiences that are gruelling and hazardous – occasionally life-threatening – at the time, but entertaining in the recounting after the event. Alcoholics Anonymous and Narcotics Anonymous have a different phrase, 'Good Anecdote, Bad Reality', which they use to refer to the addict's frequent perception that there was something exciting and special about them and their behaviour. Much of Michael's life was lived in this zone, a reckless, dark and dangerous place where, on the occasions he survived – which he did until the one sad night he died aged 38 – he would at least have the anecdote to share, embellished each time in the retelling. As Type Two Fun so often is.

I've long held the opinion that boat owners are addicted to Type Two Fun. No expedition on a boat, whether a small dinghy or a yacht, ever fulfils the crucial element of appeal for the sailor, whether captaining it or not, if the trip progresses smoothly as opposed to when there is a major mishap. The triumph over adversity is part of the process. A boat throws up an endless number of challenges to be overcome. Can it be manoeuvred into the narrow space in a harbour? Is it possible to anchor close to shore but avoid the rocks? Has the sat nav gone on the blink? And can you combat the change of direction the wind is about to take and mess everything up? If there is no opportunity to demonstrate skill in overcoming these issues, the boat has much less appeal to the sailor.

It's always struck me as interesting that many very wealthy characters choose boats as their plaything of choice. Men – and it is usually though not exclusively men who buy superyachts – have a large degree of control over most of their existence, but the one adversary they are always at the mercy of is the weather. They are as obsessed with their weather apps as with the Dow Jones index.

No matter the size of their boats, the weather is the master and even the best laid plans will be scuppered by the wind direction. Captains of industry who have constantly to swivel their business in reaction to events will be placidly accepting of not being able to leave Mykonos, for example (where the winds are often an issue), for another island on the day they wish. Being in the hands of the natural world must, I have concluded, give them a certain relief from being in control. They will spend hours regaling those around them about how they had to adjust to the weather and their triumph over any manner of nautical adversity.

On a more pedestrian scale, most of us have experienced testing times which have become favourite stories. After all, when everything goes according to plan, there's no drama to be had in the retelling.

A few years back, we rented a beautiful house on the Greek island of Evia. It was a series of whitewashed cubes on a hillside high above the road and the sea. The first few days were everything a holiday should be – friends joined us and we took turns to cook, spent late afternoons down at the beach bar, and relaxed to read or chat. One evening we were all gathered on the main terrace after dinner to drink wine and ouzo and, encouraged by the alcohol, to play games. Across the water, we could see the flashing lights of an electrical storm and hear the occasional vague rumble of thunder, but it was many miles away on the mainland and didn't concern us.

Eventually, we went to our bedrooms, some in the little cabins on the hillside and David and I in the master bedroom at the top of the house. We locked the metal and glass doors and bolted the windows to stop any rattling. As the night progressed, the storm arrived. The doors and windows crashed in the wind and the rain was relentless for hours. After little sleep, we saw the daylight seep through the cracks around the windows, and I dared to look outside. It was an apocalyptic spectacle.

The hillside behind the house, which, like so much of Greece, had lost a huge amount of vegetation in the forest fires of the previous year, had become a mudslide; rivers of mud were not only leaking under the doors into the house, but running in torrents down the slope where the guest bedrooms had been built. We were fortunate to have the one room not at ground level, but our guests woke to find themselves and their belongings knee-deep in mud. The rocky track up to the house, difficult to navigate at the best of times, had turned into a swamp, effectively marooning us from civilization. And heavy rain continued to fall from the impenetrable grey sky above.

It was a brutal few days and, after the initial Dunkirk spirit, tensions began to emerge among the guests, marooned in a cold and sodden house as the rain poured down and exit routes to the much-longed-for airport were unavailable. But hey...once we eventually all got back to dry land, it made a great story. And it's a story I've heard both them and us tell. Quite often.

Working on a fashion magazine was filled with episodes of Type Two Fun. The best stories and photo shoots are often difficult to pull off, with numerous logistical issues alongside the actual photography. It is the alchemy between the many people involved – the stylists, the photographer, the production team, the model – that turns an image from something pedestrian into something memorable.

Back in December 2016, I was keen to use a young Russian photographer and fashion designer called Gosha Rubchinskiy in the magazine. His images were stripped of any glamour and portrayed a dour yet youthful vision of Moscow – I thought it would be interesting to contrast his reportage style with high fashion. Rubchinskiy's work was defined by his gritty street style and aesthetic, not usually found in magazines like *Vogue*.

The plan was to pair a hugely successful freelance stylist, Joe McKenna, with Gosha, since in terms of taste, Joe liked a similarly apparently minimal approach, though his shoots were always hugely complex. After much debate and negotiation, dates were agreed with everyone in Moscow. Cue a series of disasters.

We wanted to get the story done before the Russian winter was at its worst, but Joe was diagnosed with a health problem. My first uncharitable thought on hearing the news was that this was an extreme way to avoid having to go to Moscow, which was even then at minus 15 degrees Celsius, to shoot with a photographer he had never worked with. But he appeared in the office, clearly very sick and pale, and agreed to try to find a new date early in the new year. By late January, everything had been lined up except that Joe wanted to change his flight: he didn't want to fly on a Boeing 777 because that is his unlucky number. He moved to another flight.

Gosha didn't usually shoot fashion, so finding a model

that everyone agreed on had taken some time. Eventually, our bookings editor Rosie Vogel had confirmed the choice, but when the team arrived, they discovered the Russian model everyone had agreed to use had disappeared from her hotel room in the city. She had flown in from New York that morning and checked into the hotel, but was nowhere to be found. Her agent, who apparently spoke no English, was contacted and the team were told that the reason for her sudden disappearance was that she had had to rush to Siberia, where her grandmother was very ill.

A replacement was scrambled from the agency, but Gosha and Joe didn't like her and now the only model whom both found suitable was a male Russian ballet dancer. By this time, I was becoming desperate about this story. I had wanted to use Gosha because of his reportage style, but I did need some girls in clothes.

The tension was very high throughout, as this whole endeavour had cost a lot of money and time to put together. The original model remained MIA and when the team returned to London, a different story emerged. Rosie told me that, far from visiting a sick grandmother, this poor girl had been whisked out of Moscow, by what was known as her 'mother' agent, to fly to Sicily for a shoot for Russian *Vogue*. Clearly, her agency felt that the Russian edition of

Vogue was more important to them than we were.

What kind of a business would consider flying a girl across the Atlantic to Moscow and then immediately out to Italy within 24 hours? It was irresponsible and inhumane, but that behaviour was nothing to do with us. At the time, the model's disappearance was a logistical nightmare, throwing the balance of a whole issue into chaos.

Now, looking back, it's a poignant story about the dark side of the Russian modelling business of the time. I draw on this memory to illustrate the sort of problem that was often the background to the beautiful and compelling fashion images in the magazine. And it is, of course, another illustration of Type Two Fun – a high-wire act, ghastly at the time and rather fascinating as a story.

Perhaps it is because I am by nature nervous and cautious that I find myself attracted by characters who are the opposite: gamblers, drinkers and wild cards who regard risk as just as essential to their existence as oxygen. It means that I, and others like me, can feel the frisson of the danger, excitement and difficulties, but unintentionally and at a distance. We may be able to tell the stories, but we aren't the players. We can share in their losses and winnings, but we never choose to play the hand ourselves.

Heels Matter

The kind of shoes we wear can influence our mood more than any other single item of clothing.

The 2001 autumn season of fashion shows was dramatically disrupted by the 9/11 attacks on New York. Many fashion editors and buyers from across the world had been flying out to the city when the planes struck the Twin Towers. Some were either diverted home or landed in Newfoundland or Nova Scotia.

Fortunately, I wasn't among them and instead spent that terrifying moment watching the horror on a small black and white television in the basement of a house in southern Spain, where I was on the last days of a holiday.

Understandably, in the light of what had happened, there was much discussion over whether the shows not only in New York but also coming up in Paris, London and Milan should continue. But they did. Everyone agreed that despite this horrific event, as much as it was possible, business had to proceed as usual.

Over the years, I have concluded that the Americans

are by far the most risk-averse and anxious of nations in a manner that might be comparable to the way that many of the counties with the highest Brexit vote in the UK were those exposed the least to an immigrant population. Less than half of American citizens possess a passport, while many have never left their huge country. Isolation highlights the suspicion of what dangers foreign places and people might bring.

Attending the European shows after New York obviously had to involve flying across the Atlantic at a time when every day brought rumours of new attacks being planned and lethal anthrax spores had been found in packages mailed to various American figures. When, a few weeks later on 7 October, Operation Enduring Freedom was launched by a US-led coalition attacking Afghanistan, many of the Americans who had braved the journey immediately attempted to book flights home. Never had abroad been more daunting to Americans.

Those who remained were determinedly attempting to get hold of Cipro, an antibiotic used to prevent anthrax infection that had rapidly become out of stock in the US. In Milan, their Italian drivers were spending as much of their time helping them get prescriptions from the city's pharmacies as they did ferrying them to and from the shows. It was a nervous and uncertain season, with the catwalk and the clothes providing the thinnest veneer above a communal apprehension and fear bubbling below.

Amid all this febrile angst, the shoe designer Manolo Blahnik was holding his usual showroom appointments in the city where his new collection of exquisite shoes encrusted in gems and covered in brilliant coloured satins and polished leathers was on display. If there is a single person responsible for the enduring appeal of high heels, it could be said to be Manolo. I've written before – but it's too good a line to leave out here – that if God had intended for women to wear flat shoes, he wouldn't have invented Manolo Blahnik. What Manolo near-miraculously achieves is comfort no matter how high the heel. Comfort and high heels are not a given.

Manolo understands the exact relationship between the gradient of the slope of the foot and the sole, so that the wearer is never in danger of being unattractively and possibly precariously tilted forward. His shoes have a sensuality rarely if ever matched by another shoemaker, with their delicate but always robust straps and curve at the back of the heel. It was Carrie Bradshaw in *Sex and the City*, desperately pleading with a mugger demanding her expensive Manolo Blahniks – 'Please, sir, they are my favourite pair' – that brought the designer international fame outside the elite shoppers who could afford his work.

In the showroom, Manolo showed me a titanium stiletto heel, less than a centimetre wide, which he was particularly proud of. I marvelled at its almost impossible slimness and asked how it was selling.

'The Americans are so *conservative*,' he said, in his distinctive accent, which, even after decades living in the UK, can still be an impenetrable gabble of Canarian Spanish. 'George [his colleague] says I can't include a heel like that now. It won't get onto the airplane,' he explained sorrowfully. It was a mark of how the new terror about flying was impacting the most unlikely of activities, adding increased doubt about what you could and could not travel with. Would women want to pack a pair of shoes that might show up on the scanner as a lethal weapon? A few days, later I told a friend of mine working on the *Daily Telegraph* this anecdote, which generated a story with the headline 'Killer Heels', words not particularly appreciated by the Blahniks at that time.

High heels are one of life's big divides. There are some women who will never wear them and regard them as uncomfortable, impractical impediments to their existence, which is certainly one way of looking at them.

Others, and I am one of them, regard them as an invaluable component of my life in the same way I do Bob Dylan's songs and Miss Dior Eau de Toilette Originale.

Heels make me more me and have done so since I discovered, at the age of 13, that after years of always being the tallest child in my class, I was now one of the smallest. This dawned on me when I opened the front door to Julia Farrington – who, due to being short, had been one of those I regarded as faintly lesser beings – and realized she was taller than I was. It was a sobering and memorable moment.

Height matters. It's why parents indulge in the foolish practice of measuring their children's growth with pencil marks on door frames, thereby inducing a level of competition among them which they are powerless to do anything about. Nobody wants to be the lowest notch.

We live in a world where it is regarded as superior to be tall, a state of affairs that encourages the so-named Napoleon complex among short men, driven to prove that their lack of height is not a limitation – think Putin, Sarkozy, Winston Churchill as just a few examples. Short men packing a big punch. That may or not be true, but having conducted an entirely unscientific survey of mixed-sex couples, I've concluded that short men are frequently attracted to tall female partners, while unusually tall women, fortunately for the happiness of all concerned, appear to enjoy the company of shorter men – Penny Lancaster and Rod Stewart, Sophie Dahl and Jamie Cullum, Tom Cruise and any number of his partners, including Nicole Kidman. But why this should be I have yet to work out.

Height, though, isn't necessarily only a factor in appearance. It can be practical, as I learned when I was once asked to deliver a speech celebrating the 300th anniversary of the Worshipful Company of Pattenmakers in one of the City of London's great livery halls. A patten is not, as I originally thought, anything to do with dressmaking but instead a wooden heeled construction designed to be worn over shoes to literally raise the wearer above the muck and dirt of the streets. As the streets became cleaner and paved – by the Guild of Paviers – these pattens eventually became redundant, and now the Pattenmakers company supports the craft of shoemaking.

We think of shoes as a fashion accessory – or possibly in the case of sports or wet weather a purpose-built garment – but more importantly, shoes also carry us metaphorically and emotionally into different places. The kind of shoes we wear can influence our mood more than any other single item of clothing.

We put on our dancing shoes to celebrate. We kick off our shoes to relax. We slip into slippers, an action which requires no effort and often marks time when we are making no effort. Heels require a commitment to wearing them and even an element of privilege.

Wandering around town in the rain is unlikely to work with a pair of delicate high-heeled court shoes. When I was at *Vogue*, I rarely used the Underground as transport because I didn't have to. I had the use of a hire-car account and a company car, but there was another reason. I had a residual claustrophobia dating back to my twenties that made tubes and lifts difficult. But after I left that job, I realized that if I didn't want to bankrupt myself, I would have to get to grips with public transport.

At *Vogue*, I usually wore high heels – most often 95mm white patent shoes made for me by Manolo. Life is different away from the *Vogue* offices, and my days are now often spent scurrying around between place to place in a way that means this type of shoe is not ideal. In the early days of my new world, I hadn't reckoned on how impractical my high heels were on escalators. As well as having to stave off a panic attack, the first time I braved the Tube, my heels stuck terrifyingly in the moving grid. As the staircase reached the top, I was to be found barefoot, tugging at my white patent shoes, which had to be levered out, causing chaos behind me.

In March 2020, eighteen-and-a-half years after the attack on the Twin Towers, a global pandemic was announced. Literally overnight we were grounded. Offices were closed, parties were outlawed, travel was almost impossible and our high heels were left stranded in our wardrobe. High heels are for going places and, with nowhere to go, we swapped them for trainers or Birkenstock-style sandals to go nowhere in. There may have been some who still wore their heels around the house, but in general the world as we knew it changed and went totally flat.

Yet the wearing of heels, like most other things, doesn't remain the same. Now, several years later, heels have snuck back in. It could be argued that in time of economic insecurity, heels are more popular – the late 1920s, when Wall Street crashed, the 1970s, when the glam-rock platform ruled and now, as the prospect of global recession hovers above us. Heels can encourage you to rise above things. Despite the ubiquity of the trainer, there is nothing quite like putting on a pair of heels to make you feel purposeful, to make you stand straighter, to literally put your best foot forward.

The Stick Insect Theory

There is an almost indefinable point when something slides from the desirable, known only to a few, to being known to more of us and in turn becoming less desirable.

My first encounter with a stick insect was in a large house in the Oxfordshire countryside lived in by the Labour politician Richard Crossman and his family. It was in the early 1960s when, on school holidays, we children were taken to the houses of parental friends and left to 'play' with their children, usually in badly lit rooms of old toys.

Often this would be an unsatisfactory experience – just because children are of similar ages, they are no more likely to find interests in common than adults of the same age – but on this occasion, it was different. The Crossmans' son Patrick, who was about the same age as me, introduced us to his new pets, a couple of stick insects. These were thoroughly intriguing in their ability to adopt the camouflage of short sticks, mimicking the dark branches in their glass jar. Until we eventually spotted them move, we couldn't tell them apart from the wood. We had never come across such things, but shortly afterwards, it seemed that stick insects were everywhere. Other children had them as pets along with the more usual rabbits and goldfish, and briefly our lack of owning them was as appalling a gap in our existence as not owning a smartphone is now for teenagers.

Had they always been so common or was it simply that they had escaped my family's attention? This phenomenon of not having heard of something and then finding that it, whatever it might be, crops up all over the place almost instantly became known in our family as the Stick Insect Theory and continues to be referred to as such.

The Stick Insect Theory came to my mind the other day during a discussion of quarter-zips. A few weeks earlier, a friend had told me that the only thing her 12-year-old son had asked for that Christmas was a quarter-zip and she couldn't find one anywhere for his age group. Until then, as with the stick insect, I had not heard of quarter-zips as a fashion trend, although once I had, I realized I was steeply behind the curve on this one: discussions of the merits of quarter-zips were all over the internet, even if they could not be found in the London shops my friend was trawling. Should you be one of the few people who doesn't know what the term applies to, a quarter-zip is a sweater which zips down from the neck to well below the collar bone but still above the ribs.

Over the next couple of weeks, I kept hearing the term. An article in the *FT* recommended copying Prada's last menswear collection that featured quarter-zips, although on the catwalk they broke with tradition and were zipped right up to the chin. A few days later, *The Times* magazine dedicated a full page to 'Why the Quarter-Zip is the It Knit of 2026', with a picture of actress Jennifer Lawrence in a grey number; then, in what was thought of in fashion as an influential intervention, Matthieu Blazy, the new creative director of Chanel, showed them in his first ready-to-wear collection, staged in a disused New York subway.

So when at New Year I was sitting across a refectory table in a Scottish kitchen from a young man wearing a dark ivy-coloured quarter-zip, the Stick Insect Theory inevitably bounced up.

When I asked him if he was wearing a quarter-zip, he acknowledged, in that slightly bashful manner many of us do when we are wearing something we know is just that bit *too* of the moment, that he supposed it was, but it wasn't a *real* quarter-zip. Real quarter-zips, he claimed, were worn by bankers and made of thinner wool, like a merino or cashmere. His was a bit more of a hardy outdoors type that would distinguish him from being a stealth-wealth *Succession*-type dude of the kind who took the view that only the little people wore formal jackets for work. Naturally, not only bankers wear quarter-zips, since that would hardly be the inspiration for my friend's 12-year-old son, but I got his point. At that moment in time, quarter-zips were peaking on the Stick Insect Theory graph.

There is an almost indefinable point when something – a plant, a food, a brand of scented candle, a piece of clothing – slides from being desirable, known only to a few, to being recognized by more of us and, in turn, becoming less desirable – more normal, less exotic. The Stick Insect Theory applies at precisely that point. It is at the stage of social osmosis where awareness of whatever it might be begins to infiltrate the mass, but it's still just recherché enough to feel like a discovery.

As with all candidates for the Stick Insect Theory, there is a shelf life to their suitability. Once they become part of the unremarkable everyday, the term no longer applies. It is only relevant for a brief moment and it is an entirely individual matter who and what any of us might include. There is never a common recognition of this moment. After all, here were countless people who had heard of quarter-zips months before I did and who would be astonished that anyone could regard the term as a discovery. As there were all those years ago children who knew all about stick insects.

There is also an almost impossible-to-define line drawn between wanting to keep nuggets of information you have discovered to yourself, or to share them, sometimes as evidence of your own good taste or refined knowledge. I hadn't heard of the term 'gatekeeping' to describe this wanting to hug your own secret until I was asked to contribute to an article about what restaurants and bars various people wanted to gatekeep, and not allow them to be flooded with 'other people'. At that stage, the Stick Insect Theory applied. One day I had not heard of gatekeeping, and then it seemed to me to have cropped up all over the place.

By definition, writing about what you are gatekeeping defies the object, but if nobody knows the gem you are in possession of, it loses some its allure. A huge part of the pleasure in a discovery is being able to show it off.

It was 2011 when we stayed for the first time on Hydra, the Aegean island which by then was by no means a secret, having become famous decades before through Leonard Cohen's living there with Marianne Ihlen, a relationship he immortalized in the song 'So Long, Marianne'. Even so, it wasn't like Corfu or nearby Spetses, regulars on the Greek-island family-holiday beat, and there was a kind of in-the-know aura about it. Despite being very close to mainland Greece, with no cars allowed and only reachable by ferry or private boat it had escaped becoming a major tourist destination.

Nobody visiting the island can be immune to the beauty of the horseshoe-shaped harbour with the rugged mountainous landscape climbing behind it as the boat approaches. Disembarking onto the cobblestone paths, where donkeys are laden with luggage and food – the moment never loses its impact. The island's beaches are stony and unprotected from the sun that bakes the harsh hilly landscape, and can only be reached by walking along the cliff path or by boat. During our first visit, there were few rental villas and even fewer hotels, and because this was before Airbnb, it was relatively difficult to find accommodation.

So it was rare to meet people who had visited Hydra, and those who had would display that information with a proud flourish, as did we. But by the next time we visited a couple of years later, this slightly under-the-radar destination had become the holiday spot of choice for many journalists, artists and fashion designers. It had taken next to no time for any possibility of it qualifying on the Stick Insect metric to have evaporated and for it to become simply another place to go.

Nothing could illustrate this more than the summer of 2015, when we were lying on the pebbly St Nicholas beach in the late afternoon, waiting for one of the small water taxis that regularly ferry visitors to the swimming spots along the coast from the town. In the relatively empty sea ahead of us, a superyacht cruised into view. It would have been hard to miss its vast presence, since the harbour at Hydra is not deep or large enough to moor huge boats and they were still a relatively rare sight around the island.

I remembered that the businessman Sir Philip Green and his wife Tina had recently taken ownership of their new yacht, the *Lionheart*, costing around $150 million, and although Philip was already embroiled in the controversial sale of BHS and its hugely under-funded pension scheme, I had a soft spot for him. He was ostentatious and overbearing, but during his pomp years, the whole fashion industry ignored that and sucked up to him as one of the biggest and most successful players on the UK scene. He certainly contributed to British fashion in a meaningful way, supporting many of the young designers who needed finance in the early stages of their career. He also brought a swagger to the scene that was largely missing.

Even though the full story had yet to unfold, a story that has resulted in Philip's mainly living now in a self-imposed exile in Monaco, I was still unwilling to join fully in the angry criticism, mainly because I once spent an evening with him in a Chinese restaurant in New York after that year's Anglomania-themed Met Ball. He and Tina sweetly played a game with wine corks with my then ten-year-old son, in between discussing the colour that the interior of his jet should be with a venture capitalist called Jerry, who had recently had a gastric band inserted.

So I sent him a text from the beach asking if it was his yacht I could see steaming into view. Indeed it was and he invited us to come on board. David and I arrived back at the harbour on the small public taxi, bouncing along in the wake of the megalithic boat, and after some persuasion, David agreed to join me on this foray.

Philip collected us from the quay in his tender and whizzed us out to the *Lionheart*. He proudly took us on a tour of the extravagant interiors – the mosaic-floored lift, the manicure tables by the sun loungers, the glass-fronted wine cupboard designed to show the labels of his collection of Château Pétrus, the his and hers port and starboard bedroom balconies. Everywhere there were taupe and brown towels with a lion's head embroidered in silver or bronze. We had a traditional English-style tea served with delicate sandwiches and the offer of champagne.

By the time we were back on the island, we had discovered that Kate Moss and her family were also on Hydra, anchored in the harbour opposite entrepreneur Sir David Tang's boat, where Sarah Ferguson was on board. Kate had been Philip's trophy buy when he persuaded her to design a range for Topshop.

Some years earlier, at a fundraiser organized by Bella Freud and Jemima Khan in aid of the Hoping Foundation for Palestinian Children, Philip had turned up after dinner in time for the auction and bid £60,000 for a kiss with Kate Moss. Just after he had placed the bid, pleased with himself, in his words, for having 'saved this crap auction', he realized the day was in fact deemed a commemorative day in the Jewish calendar and that, as a committed Jew, it wouldn't look good if he was seen paying for a snog at an auction for Palestinian children. So instead he donated the kiss to Zac Goldsmith, Jemima's brother. He told me afterwards that later that evening, he went to Aspinall's casino and won all the money back on blackjack. Who knows whether that was true. But perfectly possible.

David Tang was hosting a dinner at the island's Sunset

restaurant at one end of the harbour overlooking the sea and kindly invited us to join. We sat at the long table where I talked to Kate's then boyfriend Nikolai about photography. The next day, we were having dinner in a restaurant on one of the side streets and sat at a table next to the Channel 4 news presenter Jon Snow, who was, along with a number of other journalists, trying to track down Philip Green for interview. I thought of Philip standing on one of *Lionheart*'s many decks in his Vilebrequin shorts, talking on the flip phone he favoured, floating around the Aegean, as his business life was about to implode. The moment when the island might qualify on anyone's Stick Insect register was long gone. Which might too have once been true of Philip Green.

Things You Shouldn't Say

— It's so you... (It rarely is and it's usually hideous.)

— Try it in pink – I always think pink's your colour.

— You can't go wrong with... (Applied to just about anything.)

— Do you think you should try a larger size?

— I used to have something just like that.

— You're looking well... (Might I be looking ill?)

— I always knew he/she wasn't right for you.

— You do know he/she is having an affair?

— What are *you* doing here?

— Can you smell something a bit weird?

— You're so hard to buy presents for.

— Surely you remember?

— There's nothing I like more than being tucked up in bed by nine. Can we meet at 6.30?

— You were the most beautiful woman I have ever known. Of course, you still are...very good-looking.

— I'm afraid I'm not a breakfast person.

— I hope you don't mind. It's only us for supper.

— The traffic was terrible getting to you.

— I've been meaning to get in touch, but you know how the time goes.

— You'll understand when you are my age.

— I don't want to worry you, but...

— There's usually enough hot water.

— I think I've got something coming on.

— I would have done it differently, but...no matter.

— I see you've got a new haircut.

— How old do you think I am?

The Other You, the Other Me

In reality, most of us can be certain things and not others.

During February, I read an article about geraniums which suggested how lovely a display of them in pots could look in the front garden, maybe parading down the doorsteps. I've always had potted geraniums, or technically pelargoniums, but have never placed them there and was immediately taken with the idea. I was going to be the kind of person who would have a display of these flowers outside the front door – similar to those you might find outside a house on a Croatian island or southern Italian village, although I would plant them in terracotta rather than the colourful old olive-oil tins often found in those spots. It was going to make a real change to the appearance of the house in the upcoming summer.

I had never, though, bought geraniums as plug plants, as this article suggested. Sometimes I had taken cuttings from other people's gardens, sometimes just bought them from the garden centre. These small, fragile objects would demand more attention, it seemed. They needed to be potted immediately or they wouldn't survive the transplant, and then would have to be carefully nurtured before being transferred into larger pots. I had a vision of myself gently removing them from their wrapping and tenderly installing them in tiny biodegradable pots, watching over them for the next few months until they looked robust enough to be put outside. Then, if all went according to plan, I would have 20 pale pink geranium 'Apple Blossom' plants with almost rose-like petals. Despite the labour involved, the vision spurred me on and I went ahead and ordered them.

The plug plants arrived in their green plastic casing in early March and I set about the task. After shovelling small amounts of compost into miniature pots, the plants had to be wedged into the remaining space, watered and installed somewhere sheltered. As I carried trays of them into the spare bedroom – the only place I considered potentially suitable for their early life – I realized, not by any means for the first time, that I am no gardener. I managed to make a huge mess trying to trowel in the compost, became intensely frustrated by the uncertainty around the process and got deeply bored of the whole thing by plant number seven.

Many years back, I learned I am far too impatient to be a gardener, but even so, I keep hoping there has been a change. I will be that person who potters around the garden peering daily at developments, carefully deadheading when necessary, tying back and training, learning the Latin or even the household names for each shrub and climber. But I am not. Never have been and, it appears, never will be. That green-fingered character is the other me. The person who exists in my imagination.

The other you or me is an optimistic counterpart to ourselves, since it allows us to maintain a belief that it is possible, just possible, that we might discover in ourselves the attributes we don't think we have, or live another kind of life.

A colleague once said to me that I had the perfect job editing a consumer magazine, because I really believed the products we photographed and wrote about would make a difference. That was true to some extent. I have faith in the emotionally transformative power of an object, whether it's a new eyeshadow or a new car. In each purchase, we can indulge in a moment or more of belief that it offers us a route to being another person.

My wardrobe is littered with things I have bought in this way. There is a pair of brown and green velvet Prada flatform sandals that I never wear. Correction: I have worn them, but only twice and each time wished that I had left them at home. When I bought them, I had in mind the person with the shade of olive skin that gives them a constant dash of suntan. I would wear them with a pair of knee or ankle socks and bare legs, the way that Miuccia Prada and large numbers of Milanese girls manage. And that I will never be able to carry off. I had not factored in how heavy they are and also how hard flatforms are to walk in because they are flat with no give. I know I am not the person who can wear them, but no way am I getting rid of them...just in case.

There is a gorgeous Alberta Ferretti satin skirt in a blur of greens and blues and ochre that I have never, ever fitted. Alberta gave it to me and it's sat there for over 20 years because I still think I will be the correct size one day. It's not massively too small, just enough to make it unwearable, but to give it up would be to give in to the idea that I will not be that person. And there are countless pieces that I do fit but never wear because I bought them thinking in some way that they would be worn in a life they would be perfect for. Just not mine, it turned out.

Clothes are the obvious example of things that we imagine might invest us with a different personality, but they are by no means the only objects. Take the Josef Frank *Vänskapsknuten* (knot of friendship) candleholder – a recent purchase. Made of three beautifully twisted brass branches, it's a supremely elegant and well-known design, but I didn't buy it just because I liked how it looked. I imagined it at home on my dining table, which would be set immaculately but simply for dinner. The candlestick's unfussy Scandinavian perfection would add something to the evening that my old glass candlesticks, now with wax encrusted around the base, fail to do. It would anoint the proceedings and therefore me with the same kind of easy elegance. The reason for spending a substantial amount on this candelabra that I didn't need was I was hoping to reach out to the other me.

The popular contemporary thinking is that we should follow our dreams. That all of us can be any person we want to be and there is no reason to accept that we have limitations. It's an inspiring notion, but essentially rubbish. That is not to say that we shouldn't all stretch ourselves in new directions, nor that we should just accept our lot and not aim for more. But, in reality, most of us can be certain things and not others. There's comfort in knowing those limitations.

Try as I might, I will never be a linguist and can only

master the most basic elements of a foreign language. I can't sew for the life of me, although the house is littered with failed attempts at being a practical type with a knack for tapestry and knitting and patchwork, all begun in a swell of excitement inspired by the vision of the other me. Someone who will produce Bargello needlepoint chair covers. The same person who might buy an item of old pine furniture in a street market, strip it down and repaint it, turning it into a renewed, pretty bookcase or side table.

That other person who inhabits our fantasy life can be accessed in so many different ways. We read books, for example, not only for pleasure and information, but also, from time to time, because they make us feel we are something other, more intelligent, more aware than we are. Books not only furnish a room but are also frequently bought for the other you. The one who probably isn't going to read Dostoevsky's *Crime and Punishment*, but has every intention of doing so.

It's why book covers are so important in the selling of books. The plain deep-blue covers and simple white text of the Fitzcarraldo editions, for example, mark the buyer as the kind of person...well, the kind of person who buys such books – socially aware, happy to read European writing in translation, and who takes pleasure from the stylish austerity of their look on a bedside or coffee table.

Fitzcarraldo's best-selling novel *Perfection* by Vincenzo Latronico comes full circle. It is the story of a young couple based in Berlin. They are digital nomads who even design for websites about digital nomads. The book details the objects they and so many others of their generation own, describes the precarious life of freelance consultancies, and crucially skewers aspects of the aspiration to do something worthwhile to add meaning and satisfaction to life.

Perfection is a book about the person Fitzcarraldo often attracts. By owning a selection of their editions, it's possible to inhabit just a touch of the life of a stylish ex-pat couple, even if home is a shared flat in Manchester or a mundane three-bed in Walthamstow. Not free, as this couple are, to abandon Berlin for Sicily and Lisbon. But maybe one day...

One afternoon years ago, I was walking around the grounds of the Palazzo Capodimonte above Naples. It was the start of autumn and high above that raucous city, the heat was soft and there was absolute quiet in contrast with the vibrant craziness below. I came across a stone archway with a beautifully trained border of thick ivy framing it and stretching along the wall. Standing there, I so wanted to be the person who would one day own an achingly beautiful stone archway with beautifully trained ivy. But even years later, I still remember the sorrowful realization that followed. That person was never going to be me. I wasn't going to live a life with a majestic stone archway in a garden with manicured ivy.

Then again, in some corner there still lives that glimmer of hope that I might be wrong. The small chance of being the other me, the other you, never completely dies.

The Life of the Party

They have a touch of the jungle about them,
a sense that you never quite know what you might
encounter, what might happen.

In 1978, Sir Henry Keswick, the proprietor of the *Spectator*, gave a ball at the Lyceum Theatre just off the Strand to celebrate the magazine's 150th anniversary. It was a party of the kind that scarcely exists nowadays. For months, everybody had been talking about it. Obviously not *everybody*, but if you were part of a certain social milieu that mixed the London media world with the wealthy and glamorous, you were aware that this was the party to be at. It was a little like Truman Capote's famous Black and White ball at the Plaza Hotel in 1966, with a guest list that had included Frank Sinatra, Marisa Berenson, Babe Paley, Andy Warhol, Stavros Niarchos and the Duke and Duchess of Windsor. The town was humming with who was going, what they would wear and who would be taking whom.

Reflecting on the *Spectator* event 25 years later, the then editor of the magazine, Alexander Chancellor, wrote that he had reservations about the whole thing: 'Britain was in a mess. The Labour government under James Callaghan was tottering towards its demise in a mire of economic disaster and social unrest. A ball seemed to be against the spirit of the time.'

And yet, undeterred, the ball went ahead in the hope that a splendid party would be just the thing to turn around the magazine's fortunes and anoint it with a new lustre. Chancellor continued: 'The ball certainly affected the *Spectator*'s image, but in a way that was wholly beneficial to its circulation. It started the process by which the magazine was to become fashionable with the chattering classes again, a position previously held by its left-wing rival, the *New Statesman*.'

Then 21, I had no awareness of the political appropriateness or not of this evening which, by some quirk, I was going to. I don't know why I was invited – in fact, I probably wasn't – but somehow I was there. An older friend had asked me to chaperone her boyfriend for the early part of the evening, before she arrived at the party. She was always worried that some other girl would lure him away and since he was hardly a man who needed to be looked after by me, a much younger neophyte on the social (or any) playing field, her calculation must have been that

I would pose no threat to her.

I spent the day of the ball in terrified anticipation with a dazzling girlfriend, whom all manner of men wanted to take there, but who had instead chosen to go with me and the man I was chaperoning. Before the party, we went for dinner at Drones, a smart hamburger joint off Sloane Street, as you often did in those days; when it was appropriately late, we made our way to the party, where the façade of the impressive West End theatre was dramatically illuminated.

My friend and I were both dressed in bodices made from yards of tightly bound fabric which needed constant adjustment. Mine was in a peach cheesecloth that came with a matching long pleated skirt – I think from Monsoon – and, because it was always threatening to fall down, I spent most of my time at the ball in the Ladies hitching it back up. The man I was supposedly chaperoning made no great impression on me other than he was a good-looking escort and someone who paid the restaurant bill. As soon as we arrived, he was claimed by his girlfriend, dressed as a ravishing scarlet tulip.

That's pretty well all I remember about the ball, filled though it was with famous figures I didn't know and would have been thoroughly daunted by. But the girl who had entrusted her lover to me had her own memory of that evening.

Several years later, when she had left him and he then became my lover, she claimed in a furious meeting that she had known, she had always known, that she should never have let me take him to that party. Such, in her mind, was the seductive power of the ball. Despite the event having nothing to do with anything, it was the reflected glory of that night that she must have imagined showed me in a newly alluring light.

Ridiculous as that idea was, there is something compelling about parties. While they are 'marmite' – loathed by some, loved by others – the best throw up possibilities: gossip, new people, intrigue. They have a touch of the jungle about them, a sense that you never quite know what you might uncover, what might happen.

My experience shows there is almost no relationship between the amount of money spent on a party and how good a party it is. In fact, having in my career at *Vogue* thrown hundreds of very costly parties, I would say you could almost argue it is in inverse proportion. Hours spent in conversation with party planners, scrutinizing place settings and table linens, tasting spoonfuls of menu alternatives and stressing over seating plans are only going to provide the backdrop. They are not the real action.

What makes a party good for one person is not at all likely to hold true for another. They are entirely individual experiences, which is why there is only a limited effect the general display can ever have. What makes parties are the people, not the flowers or the food or the drink. What makes good parties are the memories.

There are the certainly glamorous memories, such as Jack Nicholson pitching up as a gatecrasher at one of our *Vogue* Christmas dinners, Leonardo di Caprio bringing his mother to a pre-Bafta event, and Prince and his entourage turning up at a gala I hosted at the V&A. But that is a certain kind of memory, anecdotal but not emotional.

Good parties are where things happen – ideally to oneself. The parties I really can remember are few, and generally, they are where I met someone or some people who went on to be figures in my life. I never remember a party for the way it looked. The memorable ones have often been more chaotic in someone's home, with tables laden with random bottles brought by guests. There might be a huge fight, there probably should be inappropriate behaviour, there are the beginnings and sometimes ends of relationships. These parties are those that you planned to leave by midnight and, before you knew it, the pink sky of dawn could be seen over the rooftops on the journey home through the empty streets.

The right mix of people crucial is to a party. I've long held that one of the many divides in the world is between people who are naturally hosts and those who are naturally guests. This has nothing to do with parties, but is an attitude to life. Hosts like to be on their own territory, controlling events around them, choosing who they spend time with. They rarely enjoy staying in other people's homes and regard the prospect of spending time outside their personal patch with gloom. Despite the fact that they are naturally hosts, they don't particularly like being with relative strangers.

Guests, on the other hand, are happy to abdicate responsibility to others and enjoy the sensation of being looked after by someone else. They feel enlivened by the company of others no matter whether or not they have chosen them, and enjoy another's territory and adapting to their timetable. They are happy to follow, and regard an invitation to a party or dinner or a weekend stay as a welcome escape from their own life, as well as an opportunity to experience something new. A good party needs to be stuffed with this kind of guest, ready to abandon themselves to the events unfolding.

It's no accident that fiction often uses a party as a pivotal moment in the narrative: the early ball in *Anna Karenina* where the fatal attraction between Anna and Vronsky is confirmed; the famous Duchess of Richmond's ball in June 1815, a real event but also a wonderful scene in Thackeray's *Vanity Fair*, where the Duke of Wellington learns of Napoleon's troops assembling at Charleroi; the older woman Melissa's birthday party in Sally Rooney's *Conversations with Friends*, a touchpaper moment for what unfolds in the rest of the novel. Alcohol, a sexual undercurrent, drama, conversation: parties both in fiction and in real life are where people are mixed together with unpredictable consequences. To be tired of parties is truly to be tired of life.

Snow

The room was suddenly rich and the great bay-window was
Spawning snow and pink roses against it
Soundlessly collateral and incompatible:
World is suddener than we fancy it.

From *Snow* by Louis MacNeice

In London in the last year, there had only been one proper snowfall, something other than a quick flurry. It was unexpected and began by stealth in the January darkness of late afternoon. Often when there is to be snow, the sky is a particular shade of unbroken grey with no trace of cloud formations. But not that day. There was no suspicion of its arrival. From the warmth of indoors, none of us noticed that snow had been falling for some hours, by which point the paving stones in the front garden were white and the dark green yew and box hedging was covered.

It is rare in London for snow to cover anything nowadays, but that evening, the snow managed to defeat the traffic and the inner-city heat of so many people, lights and fumes; it turned the urban landscape into a glistening monochrome, all colour bleached from it. There is a streetlight across the street from my house and throughout the night, I kept getting out of bed to check whether the falling flakes were still illuminated. It was thin and icy rather than blossomy, and not as clearly visible just outside the window as the snow of the MacNeice poem. I hoped that it would continue into the daylight and I would wake to find the city clothed in this thrilling blanket.

To be bored of snow is surely to be bored of so much that is about living. Its unpredictability, its transience, the weighty bulk of a snowball that shatters so easily to leave nothing behind are magical. And yet it's real. A snowflake, despite its lightness, can take three quarters of an hour to fall to the ground, and not a single one of these hexagonal ice crystals will ever be identical.

Snow is extraordinary. The sparkling beauty of fresh snow as it paints the landscape and turns it into something utterly strange is captured by those lines of MacNeice, which, in depicting the contradictions and pleasures and pure craziness of being alive, embody my feelings about snow.

Snow gives us a pass to another country. Life is different there. On a recent visit to Stockholm, it was snowing intermittently. The temperature hovered around minus 6 degrees Celsius, but unlike in London, which rarely achieves such a chill, walking around the city streets was energizing. There is a different kind of chill from the snow to simply the cold air – something less draining, more lively. There is the extraordinary sound of silence as the snow stops the traffic overnight, which can be more compelling than that chocolate-box image of the snowy mountains. Familiar residential streets become strange when the cars are mounds of white and the only sign of movement is the odd footprint, of some human, some animal.

Rare is the child who doesn't enjoy the snow, not only because it might give them a snow day or an early leave from school, but also because it is exciting in its ability to transform. As children, we would slide on trays down the slopes of Hampstead Heath with our father, who would drive us there in his Morris Minor, wearing the same camel cardigan with leather buttons that he always wore. As with so many instances of paternal care, it was thrilling not just for the snow but also because he was with us, rather than at his typewriter or on the phone to the bookies.

Or we would build snowmen in the square gardens outside our flat which we could stare down on from the bedroom. They were, like all snowmen, endowed by us with human qualities. They were not just giant snowballs with a carrot representing a nose, but people that we had created out of this charismatic substance. The only tragedy was they were destined to disappear.

Snow is exciting and irregular, a place where irregular things can happen. One year, there were days of intermittent snow in London, along with biting cold. The snow had lost any trace of freshness and had turned into grimy frozen slush with gritty snowballs littering the corners of pavements that had turned to ice. Snowmen in the parks were misshapen and slumped, with sad scarves left around what had been a neck.

It was just before Christmas and I left a party given by somebody I didn't know with a man I had met there to get a taxi home. There were no taxis to be found in the freezing city and we just walked in the icy cold, ending up sharing a bed in a high-rise businessman's hotel where the double-glazed, unopenable windows looked onto industrial roofs of dirty slush.

The next morning we might have gone our separate ways, but the pipes in his nearby flat had frozen and he moved into my tiny place for a couple of days. He was extremely tall and his feet hung out of the small bath, but at least there was hot water there.

He explained quite candidly that he was obsessed with an on-off girlfriend – 'a crazy actress' was the way he described her. But for a few days, it suited him to be with me. He was perfectly kind, and himself pretty crazy, spinning around, unhappy and generally drunk. And he suited me as a diversion in those days when Christmas can expose the gaps and flaws in your own existence in contrast to the perfection you want it to be. It was a relationship that only existed in the brief period we were together. It had not the slightest future, just like snow.

Is It Ever Too Late for White Trousers?

I love their cheerful counterpart to the drabness of a dark winter morning.

There are some people who never wear white trousers. They find them unflattering and impractical. At least that's what I imagine they think. And there are others, myself included, who can never find a good enough reason not to buy another pair.

Sitting in the kitchen having a cup of tea with a friend, I noticed we were both wearing white trousers. It was that point in the afternoon just before dark in early November, and outside the pavement was covered in a tapestry of sodden russet leaves while the rain rat-a-tat-tatted on the glass skylight.

I realized that my friend, like me, frequently wears white trousers, so I asked her a question that keeps plopping into my mind each time I consider them hanging in my wardrobe – is it ever too late for white trousers?

She swept it aside with a simple no and carried on with

the discussion of more pressing matters, such as our sons and whether they were happy – a subject, incidentally, which it is never too late for. Not having a daughter, I wonder whether mothers are concerned in the same way about whether their daughters are happy. But this is another point.

In the US, there is an old maxim that white should not be worn after Labor Day, in the first week of September. It dates back to the time when the wealthy would spend weeks of the summer away from the heat of the city in airy East Coast havens like Newport and Southampton, and would travel with trunks of white clothes to wear both for day and for night. White clothes were a sign of privilege – you don't do menial work in white. Others were employed to maintain them in a pristine state. Similar to the central female characters in Henry James and Edith Wharton novels, society would go about its summer business in a drift of white. Then, as September arrived, the white was packed up and the parade of the bon ton travelled back to the city.

But that was then, and such pronouncements are no longer made as to what any of us can wear when, apart from in magazines like *Vogue*, where much of the entertainment value lies in making such announcements. 'Embrace the charm of crinkled cheesecloth', say, or 'Ruffles are big news this season.' It's fun to consider these statements.

However, as the weather gets worse, the London streets grubbier, and it's tempting just to sink into the same dingy colours of the city oneself, I take another pair of white trousers from the wardrobe and persist in wondering whether it is strange to choose them when, on some level, it would be sensible to adopt the camouflage of the season.

I know why I do, though. I love their cheerful counterpoint to the drabness of a dark winter morning. White trousers have a casual quality, unlike the more corporate uniformity of black, and I enjoy their permanently off-duty feel. Unlike blue denim, there's no questioning what shape they should be: flares, barrel-legged, high-waisted, skinny, cropped – there are far less likely to be trend diktats with white trousers. I like to wear them with a black jumper or T shirt and maybe some gold jewellery, but also formalize them with a blazer or velvet jacket. They have an inbuilt confidence which means they can be worn with almost anything. To be completely honest, it's true that they are harder to wear in winter when you have to consider footwear, since they indisputably look better worn with bare ankles than with boots or socks, but that's just a small detail to deal with and no reason to stop wearing them.

On a visit to the hairdresser to get my hair coloured, Adnam, one of the assistants whose Syrian family have lived here for years, was telling me about how he thought there were too many immigrants in London. It was intriguing to hear his point of view, but as he tilted my head back a little further to rinse my hair, he noticed my white trousers. 'White trousers,' he said, with an element of panic to his tone, and covered them up with a towel. I thought he might think they were an odd choice for autumn, but of course it wasn't that. What a daft thought to entertain for even a second.

Instead they were, he told me, an odd choice when you are having your hair intricately painted with deep-brown dye to mask the grey. What were the chances of a blob of colour landing on the trousers, not covered by the hairdresser's gown? It was simply a practical observation. Of course it was. Why would he be thinking about whether this unknown woman's trousers were appropriate for the time of year?

So the issue is not whether it ever is too late to wear white trousers, but why I should continue to ask a question which nobody other than me is concerned with? Is it because, in my mind, white trousers will forever be associated with Jackie Onassis, with her headscarf and a pair of leather

Greek sandals on her feet as she walks around cobbled streets of Capri or Portofino on an afternoon sortie from her husband's massive boat? Or because they are so often picked out as a mainstay of warm holiday wardrobes?

And if I, as someone who has a very strong conviction that we should all wear what we want and not care what others think, have for some weird reason got these cliched images of white trousers being suitable only for hot weather and holidays lodged in my mind, why do I continue to wear them year-round?

That subject, unimportant as it may be, is the same as many thoughts that pop up like a jack-in-a-box in reaction to a certain sight or object or action, triggered by different smells or sometimes words. We all have them. My bathroom cupboard is crammed with beauty products and whenever I open the door, I briefly, yet again, wonder when I became a person who has boxes of pills lined up on the shelves that would have once only been filled with shampoos and suntan lotions. It's not a thought I have an answer to and certainly not one I wish to have stubbornly and continually reappearing, but there it is.

The same occurs every week as I lie on my yoga mat on the floor opposite a mantelpiece crammed with framed family photographs. There is one of me and my six-month-old son in matching brown cardigans, taken for the *Evening Standard* to illustrate an article about working mothers; an immaculately retouched picture by Mario Testino, again of me, in profile at a V&A gala dinner, any trace of lines or jowls magically removed; and one of my brother with his sweater tied around his waist, walking with my very young bare-chested son along a path in a wood.

There are also two of my father. One in a silver frame of him wearing his tennis whites, striding with all the bustling confidence I remember him carrying; and another taken some years earlier, where he is sitting in a chair on Christmas Day, curiously wearing his favourite black trilby hat indoors, holding a book of Matisse cut-outs and a bottle of champagne. And every week, as I try to get in the yoga zone on that mat with the pictures in front of me, I think what a complex man my father was, and how there was so much about him I never really knew or completely understood. How old would he have been when that Christmas Day picture was taken? I never bother to work any of it out. I just have those same thoughts each time, before I shake them away and try to focus on pigeon pose.

So is it ever too late to wear white trousers? Like so many questions one asks oneself, it's really just about the question and not the answer.

The Sunday Voice

Others may disagree, but I have no feeling for what a Tuesday is, or a Wednesday.

One of the questions I asked myself when I was planning to leave *Vogue* was what a weekend would be when I wasn't employed in the same way. For the whole of my working life, even though I frequently had work commitments on weekends, broadly speaking there was a clear demarcation in my mind between weekends and weekdays. Not least because weekends were the time I spent with my son, but also because they were free from the workplace.

Would there still be the sense of anticipation about the weekend if I was at home most of the time? And home was that workplace? Would I still treasure that sense of waking up on a Saturday morning knowing that 'the weekend' was ahead? Without the structure of the 'working week', would I get the pleasure I was used to in the weekend?

The answer is, fortunately, yes. How dull it would be if every day really was the same. The ingrained ideas about days of the week remain even after the content has changed.

I still feel guilty about lying in on a Wednesday, even if the diary is empty. Saturday is meant to be fun. And yes, Sunday is in danger of sharing the same dreary character it did in my childhood.

Of all the days of the week, Sundays have the clearest, most commonly held identity. Others may disagree, but I have no feeling for what a Tuesday is, or a Wednesday. Personally I have always had a fondness for Thursdays, partly because there is the weekend to look forward to, but also because when I was a child, it was early on Thursday evenings that the unmissable *Top of the Pops* was broadcast.

The writer Candida Lycett Green, a woman whom many of her generation regarded as the template of perfection, told me that she couldn't stand people talking to her in their 'Sunday voice' when she became ill and had years dealing with cancer. It was such an evocative description of that faintly hushed aura that can drain the life out of Sundays.

For years, I hated them. As a teenager, they had none of the potential excitement of Saturdays, when there was the likelihood of going shopping – or more accurately, looking at shops, since that did not require cash – with friends. And there might be a party, or at least a gathering of some kind that would require time in preparation, spreading on a glutinous turquoise face mask from a jar, which could be peeled off in the most satisfactory manner and was meant to diminish blackheads. The idea that a Saturday night might be spent at home with my parents was too dire to contemplate.

And then there was the relentless and unavoidable arrival of Sunday. Nothing happening apart from the ghastly knowledge that there was still homework to do and school the next day.

As a family, we didn't do Sunday lunch and although I very much admire the idea of that gathering, it's something I have never got into the habit of. Neither cooking it myself nor going to a pub and tucking into a roast (probably not very well cooked) and a few glasses of red wine. Perhaps if Sunday lunch had been a cherished social gathering in my childhood, Sundays would have a different aura, but it's hard to change the way we feel about certain days.

In an attempt to rescue Sunday from simply being a waiting room for the week ahead, I like to invite people for Sunday dinner. That way, the day is free and prevents the sensation of the weekend seeping away.

Days of the week are strange constructs, given that, without the activities we put into them, there is nothing that really delineates one from another. Months of the year are tied to the natural rhythm of the earth, hours of the day can be measured ticking by. But the notion of different days is more vague – defined only at the most essential level by measurements of 24 hours of the Earth moving around the Sun. There is no reason why Monday should be different to Wednesday. Originally named after the seven classical planets (including the Sun and the Moon), the names of the days have evolved in different languages, but most share in common either Sunday or Monday as the first of the seven days. Other than that, there is no inherent identity. The qualities that exist in the days of the week are a man-made structure and, as such, their identities are changing.

In our contemporary world, there is even less reason for the week as we know it. We can be in communication with people who are experiencing the day before or the day after us. It might be Sunday night in the UK, but it's Monday morning in Sydney. We are connected so easily via technology that anything, anytime, is available.

The other day, I was talking to my brother Jason, an artist, about when we could meet up. When was he free, I asked. I imagined weekends were best. 'What are you talking about?' he replied. 'For me, every day's the same.' But not Sunday, surely. Poor Sunday. Immortalized in Morrissey's 'Everyday Is Like Sunday'. And, of course, in Candida's much detested sad Sunday voice.

Hunting for the Perfect Suitcase

Packing for every trip remains an uncracked code, the solution always just out of reach.

Suitcases are so much more than a mere something we use to carry possessions from one spot to another. They reveal our attitudes as travellers – how much we like to bring of ourselves when we move location. When we pack, the luggage we choose is where we deposit expectations of the place we are visiting and what will happen to us there. The load within is far more than clothing.

So, crucially, our suitcases tell us an awful lot about ourselves, which results in there being no shared ideal of the perfect suitcase. Mine shimmers appealingly somewhere in my imagination, but is as yet undiscovered, even after years of travelling and packing experience. It's simple to know what it should be, but for some reason, not so simple to find. It should be light and move easily around, yet able to take a large amount of all manner of stuff – clothes, cosmetics, shoes, books, painting equipment, playing cards. If you only need to travel with clothes, packing is a kid's game. When I travel, I have to take home along with me.

My father was a man who always carried two large, old-fashioned suitcases stuffed mainly with newspapers and everyday medical preparations such as aspirin, throat pastilles and Savlon to travel from London to Oxfordshire for the weekend. Despite the journey being only around 80 miles, he regarded those items as essential. Clearly, he has remained a powerful influence on my own packing habits.

He was also a man who, having left his Canadian homeland for the UK, saw little point in travelling anywhere else ever again. 'Why would I want to spend lots of money to be less comfortable than I am at home?' was his response when we would ask why we never travelled to different destinations abroad for holidays as children. We also had a suspicion that his idea of hell would be to be compelled to spend a fortnight on a sunny beach with his family and no work.

For years, though, on a more practical rather than emotional level, it was my late American aunt Constance who remained my packing North Star. Her view was that if you were checking bags in on an aeroplane, you might as well take as much as you wanted; she travelled in Elizabeth

Taylor style, laden with luggage. I would be summoned to help close her many large cases by sitting heftily on them in her London hotel suite when she came to this city, or in her bedroom in LA as she was on her knees tugging at the zip for her regular journeys to New York. Her original massive load would have been added to by frequent shopping trips wherever she was. Harrods nearly sent out a guard of honour to greet her when they heard she was in town. I think of her every time I am similarly tugging, wondering whether this might be the occasion when the case finally breaks.

For a naturally heavy packer, it's helpful to feel free to stuff everything you might conceivably need into the case rather than embark on a stringent edit. Even though, despite this attitude, it is still inevitable that some essentials such as phone chargers or anti-mosquito spray will be left behind. I lost count of the number of times I travelled for work and left behind my underwear and tights, but it does limit some of the stress of packing. I know women (never men) who start packing a week in advance of leaving, their bedroom floor covered in ever-growing piles to be slimmed down as the days pass. Or people who lay everything they intend to take out on the bed and then rigorously remove a third of it.

But this attitude to go big or not at all undeniably has something to do with a degree of anxiety about the trip, no matter how short. Anticipated illness being the leading culprit. And this multiplied once I had a child. I wouldn't dream, for example, of leaving home without taking basic medical supplies: Paracetamol, Gaviscon, anti-histamines, A. Vogel Passiflora remedy (and Xanax, should that not do the trick).

Although many of my travelling companions over the years have watched what I am stuffing in and remarked, 'They do have chemists in Rome/Mumbai/Prague...you know'; this is no reassurance. Yes, there are pharmacies all over the world and many far better supplied than the local chemists here, but even so, there is nothing worse than waking in a hotel room at night suffering from a bad stomach and counting the hours till said pharmacy opens somewhere in the vicinity and you can get hold of some soothing medication. And what if there is no pharmacist? Relying on unknown pharmaceutical availability is immensely stressful.

And as for the tyranny of the capsule wardrobe, why succumb to the limitations of that dreary neutral palette that will mix and match with one pair of sandals to wear in the evening, when throwing in pieces that you enjoy wearing but that don't 'go' together can be much more fun? Why condemn yourself to life without enough holiday paperbacks that will get smeared with suntan lotion but that can be read so much more easily than an e-reader when lying on the beach?

Even so, I can appreciate from a distance the appeal of 'carry-on only' and on the few occasions I have managed to travel in this way, I have found a real joy in stepping off the plane and straight out of the airport rather than enduring the nerve-racking wait and worrying whether your luggage will appear on the carousel.

A few years ago on a holiday in southern Italy, Bernadette, an American staying in the same house, told me she had worked out the perfect travelling kit. She was a frequent traveller but never checked luggage either flying within the States or abroad, and swore by a soft Patagonia Black Hole bag with two compartments that opened out flat. This she supplemented with a backpack, also I believe by Patagonia. Bernadette appeared for dinner every evening in a different dress, along with a variety of dresses and trousers and shorts for the day and an enviable range of swimwear. She had managed to swerve the tedium of the capsule wardrobe and when she showed me what she had hanging in her bedroom cupboard, I saw that it was satisfyingly full with about as many options to choose from as I, who had arrived with a huge suitcase.

As with so many recommendations, as soon as I got home, I investigated the Patagonia range, hoping that if I bought exactly the same case, I would acquire the same ability to travel with a vast number of clothes in such an adaptable carry-on piece of kit. But when it came to the moment of buying, I just lost the faith. I was self-aware enough to realize that, no matter how wonderful the case, I was never going to be a carry-on type. The Patagonia bag would just be another piece that would gather dust up in the loft, staring back at me reproachfully, as once again I chose to pull out the big, bulky version stored alongside it for my trip.

Already in the loft there are any number of cases: a smallish hard-shelled blue from the millennial favourite Away, which I can just about manage a weekend with; one hard-framed monogrammed Louis Vuitton and one red leather Prada carry-on, both trophies from my *Vogue* days. There are two larger soft-cover Eastpak cases in different sizes, which have travelled around Europe with me for at least a decade, as well my most recent purchase, a stiffer but lightweight green Samsonite which has far too few compartments and zero appeal on the looks front. So I am not short of choice. I have cases for every occasion. And yet packing for every trip remains an uncracked code, the solution always just out of reach. I approach the task with both trepidation and confusion.

There are many other frequent travellers who manage this task seemingly unperturbed and are able to pull a small carry-on together at the last minute if necessary. I asked another friend of mine, Ashley, for her tips. She's scarcely ever off a plane, whether heading to Vienna or Amsterdam. Her most useful information was that, despite being an exercise freak, she never took a specific pair of trainers for work-outs and would just use whatever soft shoes she was wearing. Some might see that as a relatively inconsequential piece of advice, but I regarded it as a major breakthrough. Many are the times I have struggled at the end of packing to fit in a pair of running shoes (in the misguided belief that I might actually go for a run on holiday). Yes, you can always wear them on the plane, but that instantly adds a package-holiday-to-Disneyland element to your travelling look.

Years of business travel should have turned me into a packing supremo, but have made little impact. Frequently, the massed bands of fashion press and buyers would take the same flight, and there was a time – probably during the early 2000s – when there was an element of status in landing in one of the fashion-week cities and waiting at the baggage carousel with a porter ready to carry your capacious luggage on a trolley to your waiting car. Or in having another such porter greet you off the train. Only the little people travelled with small cases. Even more superior was to get luggage FedExed out in advance, ready to meet you in the hotel on arrival. Certainly, you were not to be seen lugging your own wheelie across the arrivals at Milan's Linate.

As an example of the kind of luggage thought appropriate for leading fashion magazine editors, Donatella Versace once generously sent me a Versace suitcase in brilliant turquoise leather trimmed with their famous Medusa logo, large enough to take several fur coats, should they be the kind of thing I might take on a trip. You would have needed one of the bodyguards she understandably travels with to lift the whole thing once filled.

If the perfect case remains elusive after all this time, that does not mean I've given up the search. Recently, someone I was travelling alongside was using a case by Carl Friedrik. It was a very smart aluminium number with leather trims. These cases are not cheap, but they tick the stealth-wealth box for travel. Although the brand was launched by two Swedish brothers, it is now based in Britain. This is not something they promote on the website, because I imagine that, with suitcases marketing, as with everything, there is a value in the backstory – and Scandinavia has a chic, minimal style which should appeal to their demographic in ways that a journey to, say, Bath or the Lake District does not. If you are the kind of intrepid person who might be hiking in the Atacama desert, this is not for you, but my friend Tricia, another regular traveller, says this case has changed her life. She just loves it. It goes everywhere with her.

I understand that. Love would not be too strong a word if I ever found that perfect suitcase.

Picnics

A picnic needs to be an exercise in indulgence, not stoicism.

In the late 1980s, three years before I became editor of British *Vogue*, my job was features editor on the magazine. This had nothing at all to do with the fashion, but instead involved looking after all the subject matter that dealt with the rest of life – cookery, arts, interviews, gardening, health. I liked to try to come up with ideas that had nothing to do with the current movies or plays or art exhibitions which every newspaper and magazine would be reviewing, and for one issue, I suggested a piece about famous groups of friends that could be illustrated with great pictures. It was headlined 'People Like Us'. The idea was triggered by a favourite black and white photograph of mine, *Picnic*.

Taken in 1937 by Lee Miller, the model turned photographer, it is one of a series that shows the artists Nusch and Paul Éluard, Miller's husband Roland Penrose, the surrealist Man Ray and his beautiful Creole friend and model Ady Fidelin, in Mougins, then a fashionable area in the South of France. They lie languidly in a woodland clearing, on cushions propped up against huge logs from the trees around, a low table laden with plates and bottles in front of them. They are all young, beautiful, seemingly happy, relaxed. They appear unaware of the war to come in only a couple more years. The men are clothed in casual shirts, their hair short in the style of the day. The women are naked from the waist up, their small breasts suntanned and exposing the slightly paler skin of a bikini top worn on other days.

A colleague of mine some years later at *Vogue* also loves this picture and owns a copy of it. She loves it so much that she took it to the cosmetic surgeon she had employed to reduce the size of her breasts. She wanted the surgery, she said, to make her *feel* like the women in the picnic photo.

I so know what she meant. The carefree lack of restriction that permeates the picture, including Nusch and Ady unburdened by large breasts that needed to be tethered in a restrictive bra, is palpable. But I suspect that my colleague was also reacting to the delicious feeling of relaxation, warmth, friendship and youth encapsulated in this photograph, much of it invoked by the pleasure of eating and drinking in the fresh air and by the informality of the picnic.

Even though we all have different definitions and experience of picnics, rare is the person who doesn't get a childish frisson of excitement at the thought of one. In children's books, they often represent freedom – an escape from the grim authority of adults, from the restriction of having to sit at a table with a plate of food in front of you that you have been ordered to finish. Every scrap. I remember being told to think of the poor children of Biafra, which was then suffering with terrible famine, and Bangladesh, decimated by floods, when I didn't want to eat my ham or something equally distasteful to me. There is no sitting in front of a plate of unwanted food at a picnic.

The concept of the picnic, as opposed to simply food eaten outdoors, began where food was brought to an occasion by a number of people and served haphazardly. Something thrown together. The French *pique-nique* was an early term that gained popularity in this country as a different, new form of socializing. Picnics were part of the 19th-century trend for romanticism. At its peak, as towns, villages and cities were changing forever as the Industrial Revolution brought urban living with its factories, crowds and mass production, all things rural were feted. The shepherdess crook became a favourite accessory in the popular fancy-dress balls of the time, Constable painted

'The Hay Wain' with its vision of idyllic Suffolk country life and poets chose nature as their subject: Wordsworth's crowd of golden daffodils, for example, and Keats's 'Ode to a Nightingale'.

Certainly by the mid-1800s, the picnic had become a favourite subject matter for artists. Claude Monet offers a sumptuous *Déjeuner sur l'herbe* with a large group we suppose to be of friends, gathered in a glade under trees, the women in extravagant wide-skirted dresses, the men in long loose coat jackets of casual wear, about to tuck into a splendid-looking meat pie, a whole roast chicken, baguette and wine. Only a year or so earlier, Édouard Manet had produced his own controversial *Déjeuner sur l'herbe*, with two fully dressed men lounging on the grass beside a brazenly naked women, her white skin contrasting with their dark clothes, while another woman emerges in her chemise from the river to enjoy a picnic – a definite forerunner of that Lee Miller shot. When I was first shown this picture about age four, it was not the food that I noticed, nor the fact that the central woman was unclothed, but her feet. 'Look, no shoes,' was reportedly my excited comment. As any child appreciates, not having to wear shoes is just as liberating as picnics.

As an occasional treat around that time, I was allowed

to have what was called a picnic in our flat: it involved putting a tablecloth on the carpeted floor in my bedroom and eating tea on it. The thoroughly enjoyable experience was entirely different from sitting at the small Formica-topped kitchen table where we would normally have that meal, and were constantly told to sit up straight.

Several years later in Oxfordshire, where we would spend school holidays, we children were allowed to set off over the garden wall into the fields that stretched for miles dotted with small Cotswold villages. Here we could scamper at will with picnic supplies: a bottle of Corona, a KitKat, perhaps some crisps, a Robertson's raspberry-jam sandwich. For a greedy person, it was this bounty that was the centrepiece of the expedition rather than the adventure.

And in my nostalgic memories of these picnics, it was always summer, the grass was long, there was the possibility of finding a four-leaved clover, there were streams that could be dammed with mud and sticks. There was no darkness. It was still light at night when we were shoehorned into bed, as it was when we woke.

But of course it wasn't really like that. Georgina Battiscombe opens her 1949 book *English Picnics* with this chilling but accurate observation:

> A picnic is the Englishman's grand gesture, his final defiance flung in the face of fate. No climate in the world is less propitious to picnics than the climate of England, yet with a recklessness which is almost sublime, the English rush out of doors to eat a meal on every possible and impossible occasion.

Could it be precisely because of our inclement climate that we are so fond of picnics? If the weather were good enough to eat alfresco daily, surely it would lose the appeal of that special occasion that is a picnic. Although in reality, many are the picnics we hold in drizzle and damp, hoping against all experience that the rain will hold off for long enough for the sandwiches to be unwrapped from their foil and the Thermos emptied of soup.

That type of picnic holds no appeal for me. A picnic needs to be an exercise of indulgence, not stoicism. A picnic is not about how hardy and unminding of being frozen and drenched one is, but a wonderful sense of leisure. Is there really ever a case for a *brisk* picnic?

For this reason, the picnics I experienced on the island of Nantucket in Massachusetts didn't qualify as picnics. The holiday was my first experience of East Coast preppy life. My son and I were the guests of one of my oldest friends, who had married an American man whose family owned several large houses on the island. Our days were steeped in all kinds of Nantucket outdoor activities such as going to 'the club', where the children had swimming lessons in a rather unattractive pool, playing endless tennis – the whole family had coaches – and taking lunch to the beach.

In the UK, we would have regarded the meal we brought to eat as a picnic, but to be fair, I'm not sure the Nantucket crew called them that. Extremely wealthy American financiers in their Polo shirts and khaki shorts would congregate most days on a long beach and sit in low-slung beach chairs sunk in the sand, where a single submarine sandwich wrapped in polythene would be eaten as joyless sustenance before the real action of playing volleyball or crashing around in the waves.

In the myriad of things about this scenario that don't conform to the delight of picnics is the fact that there was no picking things out from the display on the cloth or grass in front of you. One sandwich each. Job done, rather than the slow grazing that is so essential to a real picnic.

That was the dramatically opposite end of the spectrum from the approach of the original domestic goddess,

Mrs Beeton, who laid out the menu for Victorian picnics of up to 40 people:

> A joint of cold roast beef, a joint of cold boiled beef, 2 shoulders of lamb, 4 roast fowl, 1 ham, 6 medium sized lobsters, 1 piece of collared calves head, 18 lettuces, 6 baskets of salad, 3 or 4 dozen plain pastry biscuits, 2 dozen fruit turnovers, 4 dozen cheesecakes...

...was her suggestion.

Furthermore, her 'Things Not to Be Forgotten at a Picnic' included 'a stick of horseradish, a bottle of good mint sauce, a bottle of vinegar', finishing with 'take three corkscrews'. And this extract has been heavily edited down.

Barbecues, of course, are another form of outdoor entertaining that are not picnics. In her 1965 book *Summer Cooking*, Elizabeth David compares the delicious foods she and friends scooped up in their local Marseille market: 'olives, anchovies, salami sausages, yards of bread, smoked fish, fruit and cheese'. When they arrive at the designated picnic destination to be shared with another group of friends, they are 'well disposed to appreciate the sun and the sea and the scent of wild herbs and Mediterranean pines'. That is, until they are confronted with the other group's very different approach:

> One of the first things to come out was a hatchet, with which they efficiently proceeded to chop down olive branches and in no time at all there was a blazing fire. Out of their baskets came cutlets, potatoes, bacon, skewers, frying pans, jars of ice, butter, tablecloths, all the trappings of a minor barbecue.

A barbecue, with its need for organization and preparation and a controlling person manning the grill, is so definitely not a picnic.

When I was in my twenties, my friends and I were living in small London flats and frequently, on warm weekends, would meet for a picnic. We could carry our contribution to the large parks, where in the summer the grass is tall and bleached and the paths cut through like scars, or the private communal gardens attached to squares and crescents and the city's mansion blocks.

I would arrive excitedly to join a group with a basket of wine, a baguette, some rather nasty Germolene-coloured taramasalata, a blanket and cigarettes, unsure who else would have gathered at the rendezvous point. We would sprawl on cotton clothes or blankets for long lunches which would last until the plans were made for the evening. I would scurry home with my basket for a quick change and get ready to meet them later in a wine bar or at a party we knew was happening. Rarely was the rest of the evening anything like as pleasurable as that afternoon picnic.

When I first met Paul, who later became my first husband, he was separated from his wife and on 'his' weekends, we would take his two children to the landscaped gardens of Chiswick House for a picnic as a way of hopefully entertaining them, but also seeing our – or, more truthfully, my – friends. The children were having to adjust to the company of a young woman who was their father's current girlfriend, while I, in my vintage cotton dresses, was attempting to be the kind of person who knew how to look after a ten- and six-year-old. A picnic with the opportunity for them to run around made the time pass easier than being cooped up in a flat or crammed around the lazy Susan of a Chinese restaurant.

The other day, I was discussing where to eat with my friend Mary. The last restaurant we visited for pizza and a bottle of OK wine was expensive and unexceptional. Recalling this, I said, admittedly rather unenthusiastically, that I suppose I could get some food in. Suppose. A word that can be filled with so much ambivalence, which is exactly why I used it.

'Don't be silly,' Mary answered. 'I could bring something. We could get takeaway.' But somehow chicken tikka masala just didn't match with the late spring bulbs that were popping up outside in the garden and the bright light of the day, so I said, 'OK. Why don't you bring something, like...oh, something simple...we can have a picnic.'

The problem was solved. Perhaps some prosciutto and almonds, tomatoes and Manchego cheese. Maybe a delicious loaf of bread, though both of us are trying not to eat bread. There would be no cooking. There would be scant preparation. It would be easy. It would be fun, as picnics always should be.

The Pleasure of Bed

This was a bedroom I could do business with. A bedroom where things could be achieved while lolling in splendour.

When did the words 'thread count' come into our collective consciousness? Certainly for the greater part of my life I, and I suggest many, had no idea such a thing existed, but now even the bed-linen department of John Lewis – a spot I regard as far from recherché and elitist – mentions thread count as an inducement to buy one set of sheets over another. Hotels which never used to inform their prospective guests of such a thing offer their bedlinen's thread count as a temptation to stay, along with claw-foot baths and luxury bath products.

In my list of must-knows, thread counts come high in the category of needless information, but then for many, the whole business of the making of beds has become, like so much of our lifestyle-obsessed culture, an achievement in itself. And perhaps that's as it should be. Beds are important. Very important.

The first moment of getting into bed is usually the best. Giving in to the bed, letting it take our weight, submitting to the embrace of the bedclothes and allowing our heads to be supported by the pillows is a real treat. It's worth savouring that moment, since the pleasing sensation of being in bed decreases with the hours spent there, and generally by the time of getting up, familiarity with that state has numbed the pleasure. Unless you are a teenager, at which point, you appear to be almost physically rooted to the bed until well into the afternoon.

But that's if bed is considered only a place to rest. What if bed is instead a deeply comforting base for the day's activities? What if bed is just as effective a place to work as a desk?

It's taken me a lifetime to give in to the idea that bed is an acceptable place to spend time. I'm naturally a kind of wake-up, get-up girl. I live with a man whose mantra is 'Rest is your friend' and who can happily spend hours, if not days, taking up what he calls 'the prone position' in tribute to P G Wodehouse's Bertie Wooster. He may or may not be asleep, but he feels none of the sense of concern I had until recently, that being in bed is a waste of my time.

It was a photograph on Instagram of Lady Diana Cooper's bedroom that helped crystallize a new attitude to bed. Diana Cooper, after all, was the model for Lady Leone in Nancy Mitford's novel *Don't Tell Alfred*, the tiresome but charismatic wife of the outgoing British ambassador in Paris who refused to leave her bed in the British residence when the new ambassador and his wife arrived. Bed was a big thing for her.

Lady Diana's bed itself (a small double) was not the story. What was so attractive was the equipment she had around her to keep herself amused and, to some extent, allow her to get on with things. On one side was a three-tiered table piled with a rattan basket of paperwork, including correspondence to be dealt with, along with a portable radio. Crucially, a waste-paper bin was also bedside – no effective and delightful bed life should have old bits of paper and tissues lying on the floor around it.

Settled on her palest pink pillows was a bone-shaped neck bolster – fashionable at that time to make reading in bed more comfortable. On the bed were a white telephone and a pile of books. A vase of daffodils and a red amaryllis plant sat beside, on a small table. This was a bedroom I could do business with. A bedroom where things could be achieved while lolling in splendour. For me, it was one of those inspiring life moments. Cue numerous hours spent online and in antique markets trying to find a similar three-tiered table, delicate but substantial and at the correct height for a reading light.

Despite this revelation, I have not been completely able to submit to bed, although frequently, about three in the afternoon, if nothing is happening and I have nowhere to be, I will take myself off for a little lie-down. This is obviously something that can be undertaken only if one's work is not tied to office hours and there are no children to care for. A little lie-down is meant to involve a restorative snooze but invariably doesn't, since once in bed, the desire to conk out fades and instead it's possible to read, listen to the radio, scroll Instagram and simply indulge in the delight of being there.

Once bed is embraced as a place where things other than sleep and sometimes sex happen, the next issue becomes bed linen, a subject open to endless debate. At some point, we became a nation of duvet users, myself included, but in reality, they are a travesty compared to a bed made with blankets and sheets and even an eiderdown, the quilted cover that duvets have made redundant. Duvets reduce the time involved in bed-making, but they are an example of comfort being exchanged for practicality. And in a note to all suffering from hot flushes and night sweats: ditch the duvet. Make the bed with lightweight sheets and an old-fashioned open weave, technically called cellular, blanket. Layering is not just for clothes. It makes a lot of sense for bedlinen.

Back in the early '90s, Chrissie Rucker, who founded The White Company, was working as an assistant to the beauty editor on *Harpers & Queen* magazine. My brother Jason was also working there, as a more senior member of the art department. One day, Chrissie came to him and said she had this idea for starting a company that only sold white bed linen. What did he think? He replied that it was ridiculous, an absurd idea, and she should stick to the day job.

And we all know how that ended, because Chrissie has been one of the most successful female founders in the country, with The White Company now selling so much more than just than bed linen – scented candles, towels, slippers, even clothing. The White Company is a whole well-designed and affordable world. Like so many of the best ideas, its strength lay in simplicity and timing. Chrissie was early to realize that, along with our attitude to food, which has improved beyond recognition in the last 60 years, the contents of our homes have come into much sharper focus. With The White Company, she identified an opportunity to cater for this in a very targeted but affordable way.

Back in the 1960s, Terence Conran was arguably the man who brought domestic decoration to the forefront of our lives with his early chicken-brick and scrubbed-pine aesthetic, and it's not that interior decoration in terms of furniture, wallpaper and lighting was not previously valued. But by the '90s, another generation, in particular of women, was freed from the notion that it might in some way belittle them to be interested in such household ephemera as tablecloths and bed linen. Some regarded this as a post-feminist world where it was no longer necessary to fight for equal rights by being militantly against the burden of traditional female housewifery and there was endless debate along the lines of 'Is feminism dead?' or 'Do we still need feminism?'

Chrissie, with her gung-ho entrepreneurial attitude, exemplified the person she wanted to sell to. A woman who could build a huge company, but still was interested in the stuff of the home. She was far ahead of the current contemporary curve, embracing elaborate table-scaping, sofa-scaping, bed-scaping (for heaven's sake) and the trad-wife movement, but she was in the forefront of the new interest in the accoutrements of domesticity – a growing excitement over tablecloths and napkins, candlesticks, cushions and, yes, bed linen.

As it happens, last night I didn't sleep at all. For hours, I tossed around plumping up the pillows, pulling sheets up and down, wondering whether to just give in and get up and do something, anything, other than fret about why I wasn't sleeping.

For most of my life, sleep has been something that just happened. I didn't think any more about it than I did breathing. I am now aware that birdsong starts in the park outside at exactly 3.35, at first the gentle tweets of robins and tits and then, half an hour later, dominated by the cawing of a carrion crow.

In recent years, that has changed, as it does with many people as they get older. People ask if you slept well, a question that for most of my life, no one bothered to pose. But I have become one of the legions of people who spend an inordinate amount of time thinking about sleep – or lack of it. Although this is a major preoccupation, it's also one of the most uninteresting discussions available. How many times did we wake? Was it 1am or possibly 2am – hard to remember. 'It's a nightmare, isn't it, when you wake at 5.30 and there's not really enough time to go back to sleep?'

Our expectations of sleep have changed hugely over the years and the idea that we need a good eight hours of continual shut-eye is a tyranny that only makes those who don't manage this utopian ideal worry more. Far more reasonable would be a return to the biophasic sleep pattern, or first and second sleeps, a common practice from around the 16th to 19th centuries unearthed, in the late 20th by historian Roger Ekirch. Before the introduction of electric light and the more widespread uniform hours of a working day brought in by the Industrial Revolution, our sleeping practices were different. Many of us would sleep for about three hours in the earlier part of the night, wake for a couple of hours to get up and socialize, perhaps pray, sometimes eat, sometimes have sex or even do some work, and then return for the second sleep of another three hours.

An acceptance of such behaviour would suit me perfectly. Perhaps with the new emphasis on a hybrid work culture and even with the changes in working practice that AI will surely bring, biophasic sleep might make a comeback as the norm for many. And with it, an ever greater appreciation of the pleasures of bed.

Glamour

There is no such thing as hidden glamour.
For glamour to exist, it has to be noticed.

I was told a story years ago when researching an article on the subject of glamour. I asked many people what they considered glamorous and this was my favourite contribution – from the late Mark Boxer, himself a glamorous figure who was a hugely famous cartoonist and then *Tatler* magazine editor. Now he is also known as grandfather of the successful restaurateur Jackson Boxer. 'Years ago, I was telephoned by a man called Geoffrey Keating. Do you know who I mean?' Mark asked me. 'He was a kind of fixer for people, an arbitrageur, an introducer. He said, "Will you come with me to Abu Dhabi tonight?" He had three first-class tickets, one for himself, one for a friend and one for a white falcon he was taking as a present for the ruler. Is that glamorous? I think so.'

The combination of the factors involved in that story – a remarkable predatory bird, the spontaneous night-time flight to the then unusual destination, the extravagance of the falcon's first-class seat. Yes, I would still regard that as glamorous.

White falcons are the rarest of the species and are indigenous to the northern hemisphere, breeding in Iceland, Norway, Canada and northern Greenland. While the sport of falconry had been part of the local Bedouin tribes' culture for centuries before the founding of the modern-day United Arab Emirates, to own a white falcon would have been a considerable luxury at any time. They were never found in any desert environments. And nowhere near Abu Dhabi, which had become the capital of the Gulf's oil-rich territories. That white falcon would be an enviable possession for the ruler to display.

There is no such thing as hidden glamour. For glamour to exist, it has to be noticed. In his book *Glamour: A History*, cultural historian Steven Gundle suggests that the concept of glamour came into being after the French Revolution, at a time when 'manifestations of aristocratic privilege were taken over and reinvented by newly emergent people, groups and institutions'. Before that, there was certainly tremendous magnificence – displayed, for example, by royalty – but this was only seen by those inside the courtly world. Glamour, Gundle argues, came about when those excluded from it saw lifestyles they wanted to emulate.

'Glamour shone outwards,' he concludes. And glamour does shine.

While true glamour depends a great deal on the individual, many of the sparkly, obvious indicators of glamour can be bought. There are classic enduring symbols that epitomize our notions of what is glamorous – the conspicuous distancing of dark glasses, white piled on pristine white, polished black onyx, red lipstick and a scarlet gown. All are conductors of off-the-shelf glamour, along with glimmer, lustre and sparkle – a wall of polished mirrors and shelves of crystal glassware. It's why those are so often used in restaurant design to conjure up that aura.

All glamour involves the senses, particularly touch, sight and smell. Back in 1930s, the beauty entrepreneur Charles Revson coined the phrase 'hope in a jar' to describe the skincare he sold. The multi-billion-dollar fragrance industry similarly relies upon the notion that you can buy glamour in a bottle. But not all bottles are equal in the glamour stakes. Surely nobody would consider Sabrina Carpenter's chocolate-bar-shaped container for her chocolate-scented Sweet Tooth perfume truly glamorous, nor Ariana Grande's blue-bottled Cloud, which you can buy on offer with a teddy bear, no matter what other appeal they might hold.

However, everything about Robert Piguet's Fracas, the tuberose-scented classic from 1948, in its rectangular black bottle, exudes glamour, which is why it attracted and still attracts so many fans. Tragic, extravagant and uncompromising in her eccentricities, the stylist Isabella Blow would arrive in the *Vogue* offices in a cloud of Fracas that announced her entrance and stained the room with her presence.

Wearing Fracas does not in itself make a person glamorous (although many from Madonna to Brigitte Bardot wore it), but in Issy's case, it was as much a part of her truly glamorous persona as her breathy, conspiratorial voice, her disdain for restrictions of any kind, particularly financial, and her spectacular wardrobe. She would literally stop traffic wearing an array of Philip Treacy hats, knickerbockers, and crimson lipstick smeared across her mouth. As with so much that is glamorous, there was nothing invisible about her style.

When we are in the presence of glamour, it seems so real, and yet it disappears like smoke. Glamour is a twist on reality. Perhaps that is why the tragic are often invested with the chimera of glamour – James Dean, Marilyn Monroe, Carolyn Bessette Kennedy and indeed Issy. Had they lived longer, would they have continued to be regarded as glamorous, as they are now in our collective imagination?

The Germans have a phrase, *die blaue Blume*, meaning 'the blue flower', which symbolizes the unattainable, the just out of reach. *Die blaue Blume* can often be found right at the edge of the cliff, just too far to grasp, but so tempting. We often attribute glamour to people who are like that flower, or sometimes who are prepared to take the risk to gain that prize.

Glamour means different things to different people, but I doubt anyone could have failed to find it in an evening I spent during the 2007 July couture at a dinner hosted by the late designer Valentino Garavani and his partner Giancarlo Giammetti. The setting was Valentino's Château de Wideville, just outside Paris. Long lime avenues bordered the perfectly mown stripes of a lawn lit by hundreds of tea lights. This emerald carpet led to the 17th-century chateau, every detail so perfect it appeared unreal, more like a theatrical façade than a home. And so it was in some ways – a stage set for the truly glamorous life Valentino had created.

Dress code for the occasion was *tenue de ville*, which is the more elegant French for 'smart casual', but many of the guests were in evening gowns. Anna Wintour had her son in tow, Gwyneth Paltrow during her Chris Martin of Coldplay era was in a short black Valentino cocktail dress.

Although the château was sumptuous, the rooms were intimate, with low ceilings of intricately painted ancient beams and furnished with richly upholstered sofas and armchairs. Before dinner, we were able to stroll around the grounds – a rose garden that Giancarlo informed me was past its best, the fragile petals battered by the unusually heavy recent rain, and another immaculate lawn reaching out from the grand terrace with sculpted topiary placed like chess pieces on a board.

Dinner was a buffet orchestrated by Valentino's trusty retainer Michael, who piled our plates with saffron-flecked risotto, chunks (never balls) of mozzarella, prawns and artichokes. Despite the grandeur and luxury, it was a warm, friendly gathering and if I hadn't had to leave Paris at dawn the next day for my son Sam's school play, I would have stayed on with many of the other guests to dance to a DJ spinning Bob Marley. The glamour lay not just in the display of wealth, but also in a commitment to otherworldly perfection. The sights, the smells, the total absorption in a life so different from the mundanity of the everyday.

What I have not included in this account of this glamorous evening is how that day started very differently.

The first show was Chanel and, as I sat down, I noticed Patrick Demarchelier, the photographer we had flown in from New York at huge expense to shoot the couture for us, sitting with the French *Vogue* team. In the almost childish way these kind of allegiances matter in the hothouse world of fashion shows, I was infuriated, as this indicated he would be also working for them, his travel and Plaza Athénée hotel bill apparently paid for by us.

Paris is an hour ahead of London and, since I knew no one would be in the office yet, I had to wait till after the show to call the office to find out whether this was the case. When I did, there was no answer. When a member of the switchboard finally picked up, I was told that a lot of people weren't yet in the building. There had been trouble on the underground. David, whom I called, said there had been some kind of power surge, but there were also reports that a bomb had blown up a bus in Russell Square. He was trying to find out. Then the mobile connection went and shortly afterwards, I got an email on my Blackberry from my assistant Sacha saying there had been five bombs in the city and it was chaos.

At this distance from my family, I immediately panicked, first about whether my son Sam had reached school safely and then about my stepdaughter Emma and my mother, who would both have been on their way to work. What had actually occurred was unclear for hours: how many bombs, how many wounded, whether the city was locking down? It took some time for me to be certain that all my family and staff were safe amid the awful news and the dramatic falsehoods welling up in the information vacuum.

In the rarefied haute-couture bubble of Paris, the day proceeded as usual, although all the people my British colleagues and I met greeted us with sympathy for the attacks. I visited showrooms to see the designers' pre-collections (often more commercial than the autumn and winter collections) on rails, and sat on the little gold chairs for the shows, looking at astonishing dresses conjured up with exceptional craftsmanship.

Harriet Quick, a *Vogue* staffer who was on a David Bailey portrait shoot of Marc Jacobs in his Paris apartment, checked in and told me that when Bailey saw Jacobs' art – Ed Ruscha, Richard Prince, Damien Hirst – he growled with his trademark rudeness, 'You've done OK for a Jewish poofter.' Jacobs clearly didn't mind, as he offered Bailey a room for the night if he couldn't get back to London due to the disruption. It was strange to be in this luxurious disconnected world, knowing that London had suffered this terrorist attack, but instead of the dissonance I expected to feel at the Valentino dinner, it was oddly helpful to be immersed, albeit briefly, in that distancing glamour.

I rose at 5.15 the next day to get on a Eurostar to reach Sam's school play in time. The death toll had risen by 10 overnight and 700 people have been wounded. I rushed home to collect my car to drive to the school to see Sam appear as the evil Herr Zeller in *The Sound of Music*. Apart from the slimmest of smiles, he showed no sign that he recognized me in the audience, but I sat there feeling smug at having managed to get there and be a good mother.

Then I remembered the horror of what had happened in London the previous day, and felt disenfranchised by not having been present, not having experienced it, like all the other parents in the room. The privilege and glamour of the previous night, so powerful and attractive at the time, had completely evaporated and left no trace.

You Always Bring the Weather

We are creatures of the weather. Our bodies flex with changes in the meteorological environment.

'For the past few weeks, the country has been overtaken by an extraordinary heatwave. The parks and fields are scorched earth, there are dry riverbeds more common to southern Italy.

The days have been filled with unrelenting sun. We walk on the shady side of the street, searching for trees and canopies to shield us. We are all wearing hats; men of all ages have ditched their long trousers for shorts and sandals. I find this new land intriguing, with its changed possibilities and difficulties. We eat outside at night, confident that it will be warm enough, and the figs have grown brown and plump like never before, causing a constant battle between the squirrels jumping around the garden and disturbing us. The candles in the lanterns have melted into unattractive white blobs, their wicks submerged.'

I made these notes because, back in 2022, I thought I might write a book about how the weather affected us. What might emerge if I tracked it every day along with what I wore and what took place? That book hasn't been written, but it remains on the list of maybe-one-day projects.

In the United Kingdom, a huge proportion of the population is obsessed with the weather. Commenting on the day's weather is probably the foremost topic for greeting strangers: the cab driver, the guy in the dry cleaners, the postman. 'Nice day we're having' or 'Terrible out there today'. Conversationally, weather conditions are a safe bet.

As islanders, our weather is less predictable and more subject to change than that experienced on larger land masses, where there might be more dramatic events such as tornados and hurricanes, but the day is less likely to pivot from one condition to another within hours.

As an island floating in the northern hemisphere, our weather is dominated by winds: the southwesterlies, bringing rain in from the Atlantic, are the same as those that were the decisive factor in destroying the Spanish fleet during the endgame of the Armada. The Beasts from the East, as the tabloids like to call the winds that gather pace from Siberia uninterrupted by substantial mountain ranges, bring icy conditions and dump snow on East Anglia.

Despite our obsession, on the rare occasions we do have extreme weather incidents, as a nation we are imbued with a played-down pragmatism. The morning after the Great Storm of October 1987 (one of the few such incidents), I was sitting on a bus to work as it passed Kensington Gardens. Huge trees had been torn out by their roots and thick branches were lying all over the usually manicured park. The grass was completely covered with the unusual spectacle of pigeons huddled on the grass like boules. It was a dramatic sight.

Behind me came a voice in a resigned but British tone: ‘I can see it’s going to be one of those days.’

Perhaps my own fascination with climate had something to do with our father’s regular habit of dialling WEA 1212 for the weather forecast while standing in the hallway of our flat – which is how you could gain up-to-the-minute information in the 1960s. And perhaps it hasn’t, but the fact is my siblings and I are obsessed with the weather. I currently have five weather apps on my phone to be consulted throughout the day, despite the fact that at least half the time, the rain they announce will be starting in 30 minutes never materializes – rain which is never simply rain but drizzle, periodic showers, heavy rain, mizzle, a brief downpour. Meanwhile the unremitting sunshine excitedly forecast for a few days in the future appears spasmodic at best.

Only in this country could there be a breaking news story, as there was this past February, about complaints that the Met Office's reporting of the weather was too downbeat and decisive. Thousands of those who regularly check into these reports agreed that too often the Met Office spoiled their plans by simply displaying a black cloud with little blue droplets falling, irrespective of strength of the rain. This grey-black cloud was deemed responsible for the cancellation of too many picnics and outdoor activities. Nobody suggested what range of symbol might better offer the nuance to organize the day's plans. Neither did they appear to pay attention to our huge vocabulary, as seen above, employed to describe the variety of rain on offer.

A few years ago, David and I rented a small flat in the seaside town of Aldeburgh. The view from our bed was of the ever-changing colours of the North Sea that would shift throughout the day from sludge to emerald to dark grey, cobalt and even on occasion a sliver of gold. As the room faced east, we could see the sun rise over the horizon. It was mesmerizing to watch.

Just across a single quiet road was a row of fishing shacks on the shingle beach sloping down to the water. They've been there for years, mostly with the same proprietors selling the daily catch.

One weekend, thundersnow was forecast, along with a tidal surge. It sounded an exciting weather phenomenon and I raced to get there from London as soon as I could on the Friday evening. Thundersnow is when the ground is warm enough and the atmosphere cold enough to bring on a thunderstorm that lights the falling snow, causing a strangely bright sky and muffled bangs. I was really eager to experience this previously – to me – unheard-of phenomenon.

The weather all weekend was disappointingly calm, if a bit chilly. No thundersnow, no tidal surge, not even a heavy frost. One of the fish sellers on the beach told us they knew there wouldn't be any of these things since the wind had changed direction, a fact seemingly ignored by the weather forecasters. It makes you wonder why they don't consult the fishermen whose livelihoods depend on a degree of accuracy rarely offered up on AccuWeather or, as I have renamed it, InaccuWeather.

It's no accident that Burberry, one of the very few internationally successful British fashion companies, has its roots in the weather. Thomas Burberry built his business on waterproof gabardine, a fabric that could keep the wearer warm and dry. It was used for everyday outerwear, but soon became world famous. Burberry's trench coat was worn by the officers in World War I, and both the Norwegian explorer Roald Amundsen and the British Ernest Shackleton wore Burberry for their polar expeditions.

Nowadays when at Heathrow's Terminal 5, massive advertisements for Burberry and its famous trench worn by well-known British names dominate the huge arrivals hall, using slogans like 'It's always Burberry Weather'. No sooner have travellers set foot in the country than they are confronted with the idea of what is basically a raincoat as the national uniform. Just as other countries greet visitors with visions of bikinis on sun-soaked beaches.

We are creatures of the weather. Our bodies flex with the changes in the meteorological environment. Blood pressure can fall in the heat, while headaches are frequently worsened by barometric pressure, which can lower before rain and storms. The sensation of a weight on the head is not imagined and is a known factor in migraine. Joint pain may also be worsened by cold weather. In the US, the Arthritis Foundation offers a 'weather and arthritis' index.

Almost everyone living in Britain knows of the mood-lowering effect the unmitigated grey of our winter can have. People talk of Seasonal Affective Disorder causing depression and persistent gloom. In other countries, it's the annual arrival of the different winds that affects the psyche: the foehn winds of Scandinavia are said to increase incidents of psychosis and suicide; the hot and dusty conditions of the Moroccan sirocco, which many find exhausting and which affect their breathing, blow in from the Sahara; in the South of France, the winds of the equilibrium-disturbing mistral rush noisily and persistently through the olive trees with a rattle that can drive you mad. In her 'Los Angeles Notebook' essay, Joan Didion wrote of the Santa Ana: 'A hot wind from the southeast winding down the Cajon and San Gorgonio passes, blowing up sandstorms out along Route 66, drying the hills and nerves to the flashpoint... We know it because we feel it.'

In 2017, I was sitting in a hotel bar off Sunset Boulevard in Los Angeles while Hurricane Irma pummelled the Florida Keys. A woman sitting next to me informed her friend as they sipped margaritas, 'I hear they're all out of Xanax in Boca Raton,' referring to the low-lying Floridan coastal city. No surprise there. Even moderately dramatic weather conditions can induce anxiety, let alone a neighbouring hurricane.

I have several books on the subject and should you ever feel the world is going to pieces in an unprecedented manner, *Gigantic Cinema*, an anthology of writing on weather compiled by Alice Oswald and Paul Keegan, is a tremendous antidote.

During the 2022 heatwave mentioned at the beginning of this piece, numerous scaremongering articles were written and news reports broadcast, as the thermometer topped 40 degrees Celsius in this country for the first time. The same year, there was an unusual amount of volcanic activity from Etna on Sicily and Stromboli on the Aeolian islands, while the Hunga Tonga-Hunga-Ha'apai volcano in the South Pacific caused the largest recorded underwater eruption. It did at times seem the world was imploding, but I found comfort in this piece in the anthology, by the 18th-century satirist Jonathan Swift:

> The summer of 1783 was an amazing and portentous one and full of horrible phaenomena; for, besides the alarming meteors and tremendous thunder-storms that affrighted and distressed the different countries of this kingdom, the peculiar haze, or

> smokey fog that prevailed for many weeks in this island, and every part of Europe, and even beyond its limits, was a most extraordinary appearance, unlike anything known within the memory of man... The country people began to look with a superstitious awe at the red, louring aspect of the sun; and indeed there was reason for the most enlightened person to be apprehensive; for all the while, Calabria and part of the isle of Sicily were torn and convulsed with earthquakes and about that juncture a volcano sprung out of the sea on the coast of Norway.

The weather is uncompromising in the way it affects our emotions and health. There is no negotiating with it. However, in this age of real concern about climate change, there can be something reassuring in recognizing the way the weather has forever been such an uncontrollable, powerful master. As humans, we have always been at its mercy. And yet we remain who we are. The grey skies will end, the barometric pressure will lift, the wind will eventually quieten. Or so we have to trust.

Too Much Stuff

There used to be a world before we took recycling seriously. And it was, for all its sins, a much simpler world.

The Abbey Road (Brent) Recycling Centre certainly qualifies as one of the least glamorous spots in the country. Situated off the tangle of roads where the North Circular meets the A40 in North London, it inhabits one of those strange, almost dystopian areas on the outskirts of many large cities. There are no shops or private homes, no gardens or parks, just long, bleak, tarmacked roads spotted with the ungiving façades of warehouses and industrial workshops. It is possible to drive for ages and not see a single person, apart from occasionally a security guard on duty at one of the gated entry points.

This emptiness is not, however, mirrored by the goings-on at the recycling centre, which is always a fascinating hive of different characters and their possessions. Where some people enjoy going to Hampstead Heath swimming ponds as recreation, I love an expedition to Abbey Road – not to be confused with the iconic zebra crossing on the cover of the Beatles album of that name. It couldn't be more different.

Turning off into the depot, you enter the world of rubbish, with huge skips and towering metal structures. At the checkpoint, sometimes an over-zealous guy with his digital pad will scrutinize the contents of the cars or vans to check for contraband – i.e. stuff that needs to be paid for if it's to be chucked out: old toilets or garden fencing, ceiling tiles and vast amounts of garden soil. Generally, whoever is in charge that day looks a touch disappointed when he sees my usual load of cardboard boxes, old china and tin, electrical leads and cracked flowerpots, which all qualify for free recycling, before waving me into the wonderful world of the dump.

There is frequently an enjoyable camaraderie among the visitors. We raise our eyebrows and share knowing nods as we are bossed around by the team on the ground. These guys (there seem to be no women) clad in their high-vis jerkins appear to enjoy policing the site with the noisy authority of people in control of a small universe. 'The sign says REVERSE parking,' they shout, as our cars invariably pull up the wrong way round, and brook no argument as they brusquely reply 'Health and Safety' as the regulation answer to any question. We haul our loads up the metal stairs to the giant skips, deliberately not nosily examining what a neighbouring visitor might be dumping. Our rubbish is collectively agreed to be a private matter.

My wire coat-hangers are flung down next to an old drum kit, my two bags of garden soil (undetected contraband) cover a collection of London stone bricks. I guiltily fling a defunct laptop and iPhone into the small electricals in the realization that if I had spent a bit of time, they could have been usefully reconstituted for use by others.

This latest visit was on the day the results were coming through from the local UK elections. There was a lot of noisy banter, with Nigel Farage and his Reform party the main subject of discussion. 'He just want to line his own pockets,' concluded one of the commandants, as he diverted a customer from the non-recyclables to the spot designated for old paint cans. 'Don't believe him. They don't want to fix nothing,' a colleague cheerfully agreed.

Half an hour later, covered in dust, I departed with the car empty and a huge sense of achievement in the idea of my home being just that small bit emptier. And yet in spite of that, disposing of the stuff of our lives is not straightforward.

There used to be a world before we took recycling seriously. And it was, for all its sins, a much simpler world. For years, it was possible to simply walk around the house chucking all manner of unwanted bits and pieces into large bin bags. In would go old make-up (after trying to work out exactly *how* old a lipstick might be) and ancient bottles of cough mixture and Calpol. A broken radio, damaged CDs and cassettes would be stuffed into another bag, along with clothes that had shrunk beyond repair in the wash or been munched by moths. These would all be hauled out into the front garden and chucked into or put beside the rubbish-collection bin, and off they would be taken. No questions asked. No different bin days and different-coloured bin lids. I had no idea where or how the stuff went or where it was going. Its life, as far as I was concerned, ended in my bin.

Back then, the cathartic experience of clearing out was unsullied by the considerations we are now all driven by, in an attempt to remedy decades of this kind of thoughtless behaviour clogging up and damaging our planet. Landfill is one of the dirtiest words. Jars need to be decanted and washed, electricals separately disposed of, paper and cardboard corralled and hopefully used in another life. And as for plastics – not all plastics, it appears, are equal.

Some are granted higher status if they can be reused in a different form. The rest…the deplorables, well, they are unacceptable landfill.

Never before have we owned more to get rid of, so perhaps it's not surprising that the previously uncomplicated act of chucking stuff into bin bags has spawned a whole industry. Decluttering is a booming business, with companies offering not just to rid us of the pesky bits and pieces that have no obvious place, but also to provide a new sense of calm. Tranquillity, it is suggested, can be found in a neatly ordered cupboard.

That was Marie Kondo's USP. Marie Kondo, who, with her 2010 internationally bestselling *The Life-changing Magic of Tidying Up*, encouraged, if not a generation, at least several years' worth of devotees to fold their socks and jeans in a whole new space-saving way. Her doctrine urged us to examine each piece we owned and only keep those that, in her words, sparked joy. But she was wrong. What doesn't emit even the smallest spark one month can do so a year or even a decade later. The value we find in our possessions is not a static fact that can be accurately calculated. It depends on time, mood, events and memory.

My home office is an example of the quandary inherent

in deciding what to keep and what can go. There is box file upon box file of letters and cards and invitations and photos. I frequently consider getting rid of (or at least editing) them, but each time I open one up and start to read, what they spark is not joy but a whole bank of memories, often of people and times I have completely forgotten and enjoy remembering. Taking them to the tip would be like putting some of my life in the trash.

The desk is completely covered in a mixture of objects from the useless to the rather lovely. There is a miniature brass abacus from my parents' flat, a tiny oriental print tray bought in the shop at Chatsworth House piled high with loose change. There is an Asprey magnifying glass inscribed with the words MT2004, given as a Christmas gift by the photographer Mario Testino, and there are three small *eau de nil* porcelain pots on a stand, another gift, this from the artist and author Edmund de Waal after I interviewed him once. But there are also several mugs of broken pens and an old bottle of blue/black Quink to fill the fountain pen which I lost years back. Yes, that could go, I suppose, but...I do intend to get a new fountain pen.

Beside the desk, there is a sideboard covered with rattan trays that were supposed to be neatly housing different projects, but have simply become depositaries for all kinds of paperwork that needs to be gone through. So many cuttings that might be useful some time. So many print-out drafts of talks and articles that could be helpful. Each time something is chucked out, I invariably need to refer to it shortly afterwards, and knowing that acts as a major deterrent to this activity. There are family photographs in frames two, sometimes three, deep on the mantelpiece so that half of them are not available to view. But I wouldn't dream of getting rid of them.

The artist Francis Bacon once said, 'I find images in chaos.' His old studio, the ultimate in bricks-and-mortar chaos and now faithfully recreated in Dublin's Hugh Lane Gallery, is thick with paintings, rubbish, magazines, paint, easels, old cups – not an inch of space unfilled. He liked it that way. He was able to discover ideas embedded in the stuff that surrounded him. And in a small way – a very, very, small way – so am I.

But even so, every now and again, it all becomes too much. Too many books and shoeboxes, too many cracked plates and chipped mementos. Too many possessions that I carry around with me from home to home, now so familiar I no longer see them. Sometimes the mass overwhelms and, rather than these objects creating a sense of the safe space I like to think of as home, they simply have to go. The weight of all this stuff becomes threatening. Too much, just too much. And then, there's nothing quite like the cleansing experience of going to the dump.

What Shall I Wear?

Can the colour of my sweater really influence the outcome of a mammogram?

It was still dark outside, judging by the level of light coming through the blinds in the bedroom, so it was hard to know whether it would eventually turn into a bright, dry morning, which might make it easier to get out of bed. But then again, maybe not. Sometimes a glorious day only serves to reflect back the fact that one's mood is not glorious.

Whichever the case, exiting bed requires an answer to the question of what to wear. Unless we have to put on a uniform, there are few questions we consider as frequently, even though this one is so hard-wired into our days that we often don't know we are asking it.

More often than not, it isn't a clearly articulated thought along the lines of such daily preoccupations as 'What shall I cook for dinner?' or 'Is it wrong to buy cherries from the greengrocer in January, which means they will have added heaven knows how much carbon to the atmosphere in their transfer from Chile or Argentina?' (Everyone knows they aren't coming from Kent at this time of year.) Or even less daily but nonetheless recurring thoughts such as 'Do I want to be cremated or buried?'

That January morning, I chose to wear a mustard cashmere sweater with pink cuffs that I bought for £50 in a second-hand charity clothes sale. My skirt from Jigsaw was a boiled olive wool and had been one of those unexpectedly clever buys of the kind you can never predict. It managed to look relatively flattering despite the dense fabric and thick, elasticated waistband and it was warm – a trio of adjectives which don't usually denote the condition of flattering.

It turned out to be unusually cold outside, meaning I could allow myself the luxury of dark grey wool tights that, although devoid of even a soupçon of elegance, were reassuringly warm. And when I got around to putting on shoes, they were black loafers which – refer to chapter on heels – are not my usual footwear. But they, too, were reassuring for negotiating the invisible ice that had emerged even on the London pavements.

This was the outfit I chose for my relatively new, regular Zoom appointment with a therapist – a woman who has only ever seen my head and shoulders on the screen and would have no idea about the rest of me. Our relationship is purely table-top. I look at her and notice when she has styled her hair differently and what she is wearing and I imagine she does the same of me. Sometimes I think of surprising her in full make-up, jewellery and a glamorous blouse rather than the careless way I present to her from my desk every week. What would she make of that? Would she have a different idea of me? And would that affect the things she said?

Then there was a meeting with my lawyer that afternoon to discuss changing my will – the eagle-eyed may spot a connection to an earlier point here. I don't really have any idea what appropriate wear for discussing wills is, but I thought this slightly school-marmish look would signal to myself, if not to my lawyer, that I was not flighty or likely to make daft decisions.

I could have worn any number of other things that day. There was no clear determining factor as there are on some occasions when I am going for a walk in the muddy countryside or to a Christmas party or a meeting with somebody who I think it is worth presenting myself to in the way I think they might expect me to look. What is that? So many questions.

When I first left *Vogue*, for some time I would frequently change clothes in the middle of the day, unsure of how

I wanted to present myself for the different roles I was exploring. I would rush home and fling one person onto the floor and grab another. Although it might seem that if you were the editor of a fashion magazine, it would be stressful conforming to people's expectations of your wardrobe, the opposite was true. It was curiously simple. Of course at times I felt a pressure to look a certain way, but generally I was able to take the view that the job title conferred on me an authority that meant whatever I wore would be considered appropriate. It's a little how I imagine it is being a well-known cook – perhaps Nigella Lawson or Diana Henry – and knowing that whatever way you roast your aubergines will be regarded as correct. Even if some people eating might find them too sour or too mushy. This may well not have been the case, but over the years, I held that thought close and it was hugely helpful.

There are certain occasions which will always trigger doubt about the correct dress: being in the presence of royalty has a tendency to put everyone in a spin. Even the most sanguine about their appearance accept that these occasions demand a degree of commitment to looking what might be thought of as right.

In 2016, I was at a lunchtime reception in aid of The Landmark Trust, hosted by the then Prince of Wales at St

James's Palace. These receptions are always seamlessly choreographed, allowing visitors to process to the correct room while taking a little time to admire the paintings. Usually the courtiers are gently coercive and smiling, ensuring no log jams among the crowd, although once when I visited Windsor for a reception for the Queen to meet members of the media (possibly not their favourite collective), there was a marvellous moment when the polished veneer slipped. The epaulette-laden commissar barked, 'Hurry along there, we've got 700 of you to fit in', which made one feel more like a cow being pushed towards the abattoir than a privileged visitor.

On this occasion, there was no such brusqueness and small groups of people considered as those Prince Charles might like to speak to were corralled in advance by experienced courtiers who guided him to them through the crowd.

The large stateroom was packed and it was curious to see several members of my generation whom I remembered years back as sparky, even rebellious individuals now in attendance in smart suits, sensible shoes and long buttoned-up jackets – fully signed-up members of the Establishment. I was wearing a new plain grey cashmere crew-neck jumper and pencil skirt and, as I was talking to one woman I knew only slightly, she reported another guest's comment about my clothes. This other woman, herself a formidable Tory life peer who had led numerous reviews of public bodies including the NHS and the immigration system, had said crossly of my outfit, 'Well, she's just wearing a grey jumper. I suppose we're all overdressed.'

It had never occurred to me that my grey sweater was underdressed, nor that it would have that effect on anyone. I had thought I looked smart in my own way, and felt happy wearing this new purchase rather than something more formal. Added to that, I took the view that it was pretty unlikely Prince Charles was going to care what I wore, or even notice. But even so, it was one of the many occasions when I realized that my job gave me a confidence in my choices that others might not have.

Now that I am a lone ranger and no longer able to operate under the umbrella of *Vogue* editor-in-chief, working out what to wear is more difficult. How do I want to appear to others? How much do I want my clothes to reflect how I am feeling that day or disguise it?

The way we make those decisions fascinates me. My fashion director at *Vogue* was Lucinda Chambers, a woman who was then and still is never randomly dressed.

She always appears in an outfit thought through from earrings to socks to shoes, belt and shirt, whether at a gala dinner or pottering in the garden. Sometimes she starts, for example, with a pair of earrings 'and everything else is woven around that beloved item,' she told me. 'If I'm particularly happy with a certain "look", I take a quick snap. Then, if I'm ever stuck about what to wear, I have a little look at what made me happy that day and rinse and repeat. It works particularly well if you are making a dash for dinner and in a mild panic about what to wear.' This is a very different process to my own manner of choosing what to wear, when I might feel completely happy in certain clothes one day but utterly despondent in the same ones on another occasion.

A few days after the meeting with my lawyer, I was booked in for a mammogram as part of my regular post-breast-cancer check-ups. Although some people may be utterly unconcerned about what they wear for medical appointments, they always trigger my tendency for magical thinking. Will a seemingly unrelated certain thought or behaviour influence what happens? Can you harness good luck through a gesture or an object? Can the colour of my sweater really influence the outcome of a mammogram?

In 2021, when a 2cm tumour was found under my left breast, I had decided to wear a fluffy pink sweater for the appointment. I didn't think I had breast cancer, but I did have a nagging pain which, after ignoring it for months, I eventually decided to get investigated. Although I was a little uncertain about this choice of sweater, pink being the colour identified with breast-cancer campaigns, I wanted to wear something positive. Black or sludge smacked of foreboding. Anything in a colourful pattern I thought would trivialize a potentially serious moment. Hence the pale pink mohair sweater.

I returned to the waiting room after first a mammogram was performed, showing up nothing, and next an ultrasound where the probe found a very painful spot which made it immediately clear that this time something sinister had been discovered. As I sat there in that pink sweater waiting to meet the doctor and hear the news, I knew I was sliding from the holding pen of those who are well, the place we hope to inhabit for as long as possible, to that unknown territory of the sick, a journey I was unprepared for. That was the last time I was able to wear that sweater.

For this check-up four years later, I chose a striped navy, black and white sweater I had recently bought in a concept store in Lisbon and a black COS skirt. The thought behind this choice was to look a little bit optimistic without tempting fate in a riot of colour. Although I was hugely anxious about what might emerge in the consultation, it seemed essential not to allow a sartorial slump. Medical appointments are dispiriting enough without looking one's worst.

In the land of consultants, we are originally only a set of scans and blood tests. These people who hold our future on their computer screens don't know our family, our careers, our background. Apart from medical data, what they see in front of them is only what we look like, how we are dressed. The factual information they have about our health is telling a story, but not the whole story. If this is to be an ongoing relationship, I choose to believe that what we wear matters in helping them see us as individuals, not only an NHS or private insurance number. Whether or not it was the stripes – and I doubt it – I was given the all clear that time.

Zadie Smith, in an essay for *Vogue* called 'Can You Be Serious and Seriously Glamorous?', writes about how the way she dressed impacted her as she made her way as a writer. She begins by saying that 'while none of us enjoy appearing ridiculous, writers tend to be particularly anxious about "looking the part".' She goes on to describe her 'frock consciousness' when she first started teaching in Boston in the 2000s, wary of veering far from 'black jeans, black shirt and black blazer if I had any hope of my students accepting me as their professor'. But then, she became aware of the 'Carrie effect' in the States at the time – even intellectuals were seduced by the first series of *Sex and the City* – and loosened up. She changed her approach and decided to have fun with her clothes: 'Kafka in a kaftan...colour blocks for a class on *The Bluest Eye*... Essentially, my whole wardrobe was a costume.'

Zadie and I are both involved in a local food charity and I have to say that whatever she wears, even under the apron serving a hot lunch in a cold church, she looks exceptional, but that is less to do with the clothes than with her beauty. I was, however, pleased to see that at the same second-hand sale in aid of this charity where I bought the olive-green, pink-trimmed jumper, she scooped up a cobalt-blue silk evening dress for a party she was going to that weekend.

Our appearance is the single quickest way to tell others something about ourselves. It might be the uniform of the nurse, the modest dressing of various religions, the red and white shirt of the Arsenal fan. It might be wearing jeans to a wedding or vintage Pucci at the school gates.

After years of working in fashion, I conclude that there is no correct answer to what to wear. No such thing as getting it right or wrong. But there is the question of how do we feel about what *others* think of what we wear? How much do we care about that? And what is the story we are wanting our clothes to tell them?

You Can Always Leave

People say that money doesn't make you happy, but I beg to differ. Money makes it much, much easier to leave.

If I were asked for a list of the most useful things I have learned in my life, this would definitely be in the top three. Knowing there is an escape route available makes getting involved in something in the first place seem so much more possible.

Being able to leave is one of the defining aspects of becoming an adult. As a child you are always stuck with someone else's desire for you to be doing something you might not want to do, and almost certainly being somewhere you don't want to be. Parents, teachers, caregivers, siblings, even friends are capable of forcing you into someplace you have no desire to be.

I still remember the horror of having to walk across a Cotswold stone wall, which seemed impossibly high but was probably about 6 feet. I was jeered on by a gung-ho pair of sisters around my age, perhaps nine, who sprinted along it, not remotely fazed by the drop below and mocking my fear. They were not my friends, but daughters of our parents' friends and, even at that age, were more brazen and confident, which is a definition of sophistication when you are nine. I couldn't leave. I had nowhere to go.

A decade or so later, when I came across them again, they were also ravishingly beautiful. Rachel was a model and later became an actress; she has recently come to fame as a still beautiful but nonetheless grey-haired and lined cattle farmer – an unintentional poster girl for accepting the process of ageing. And her younger sister Tracey became a marchioness and an eco-activist. I have never been able to see either of them without remembering the horror of being stuck on that wall.

It took many years and many experiences of being marooned in places I had never wanted to be in the first place before things improved. As a teenager, independent movement is not a given if you can't drive and you don't have enough money for a taxi, so invitations to parties in far-flung corners of the city were one of my greatest fears. On a Saturday night, a group of us might pile into some boy who had just passed his driving test's father's car and head off to Pinner or Chorleywood or East Sheen, a long way from my home, for a party that somebody had heard somebody was giving. Sometimes they were, and sometimes they weren't. And if they weren't we would pile back and try to find another one. But when they were, the next issue was how to get away, something I was obsessed with from the moment of arrival. Departure was dependent on whoever was in charge of the expedition not finding someone to get off with in the parents' bedroom.

One party at the opposite end of the social spectrum was a Boxing Day gathering held in a Chelsea street near the Embankment by family friends. I was about 13. I tried to refuse to join my mother on this expedition, but she was insistent on my going, telling me not to be so silly. There was nothing to be nervous of.

We arrived at the house. From the outside, the first-floor rooms were gloriously lit and filled with figures. Like a horse rearing up at the approach of a gate, I made an attempt to avoid entering the front door, but I was pushed in. Before I knew it, I was handed a glass of champagne and ushered upstairs. The large room was crowded with people I had never seen before in my life – some old to my eyes (probably in their forties) and others just old enough to be unimaginably cool in my early-teen eyes. My hostess – and she was an experienced hostess who took giving parties extremely seriously – immediately took me by the arm to introduce me to an impossibly glamorous, tall girl wearing a completely transparent chiffon dress with no knickers. I couldn't imagine what I could say to someone who was able to show their pubic hair in public – I couldn't really deal with mine in the privacy of my bath.

She was called Carinthia and she looked just like a blonde Carly Simon. As I remember, she was perfectly kind but obviously uninterested in this mute 13-year-old and was soon rescued by the approach of a man called Andrew. The word suave was invented for men like him. Also, as it turned out, the words swashbuckling, rakish, daredevil and tragic. When he and his brother Randall died piloting their twin-engined Cessna from Turin, a 1988 obituary in the *Spectator* by Taki, a fellow high-roller of the time, reflected: 'Like Icarus, Andrew and Randall Crawley... always flew too close to the sun. They were reckless in the way brave, not stupid, men are, always laughing at danger and constantly challenging the gods.'

I was terrified by Andrew and Carinthia in their seemingly sophisticated perfection, and standing alongside them in this glowing room of confident chatter was the final straw. I ran down the stairs and bolted out of the door into the night and home. It was the first time that I realized you could always leave.

Being able to leave is a sign of independence. When I was younger, the ability to pay for a taxi was a measure of freedom – I guess now it would be having an Uber account. People say that money doesn't make you happy, but I beg to differ. Money makes it much, much easier to leave.

The times I have been most undone have been when I couldn't leave something or someone. These times were not to do with money but with circumstance. I mentioned earlier on the panic disorder I suffered from, which I eventually realized came about when I was trapped in something. It first occurred during my time at university, when I didn't want to be there, then when I was in a relationship that I knew I had to leave but for various reasons kept returning to, and later, when my first marriage was impossible, but more impossible and unbearable was the prospect of abandoning it.

Because of this panic, with its accompanying claustrophobia, one of the most difficult aspects of my job for many years was going to fashion shows. Not all fashion shows, but those where hundreds of people were crammed into cavernous dark spaces. As a *Vogue* editor-in-chief, I was kindly given a privileged front-row seat, frequently in the centre of the row, but much of the time, this was anguish. I would look along the row, planning how I could rush out if need be. I would scan the room for where the exits were, the same way I still do before a plane takes off. I dreaded the edgy warehouse shows in the back of beyond, where the atmosphere would be deliberately designed to incite a kind of nervous apprehension of the dark aesthetic the designer wanted to promote. Or the New York shows where we would have to cram into a cranking goods elevator to be carried up 20 storeys to where some designer chose to show, and then in order to leave have to endure a terrifying crush and stampede to get back to the street.

Making the decision to leave is the hard part, not the actual departing. That's true of many decisions, although my mantra is that any decision is better than no decision – you can usually change it. The more you consider whether to leave, the more impossible it becomes. Before I finally decided to leave *Vogue*, I spent a considerable amount of time looking at the seagulls on the rooftops opposite the flat we had in Aldeburgh on the Suffolk coast. I would see them all facing into the wind like aeroplanes in order to take off and wonder whether, if I took off, I would be facing the right direction. Would I achieve the necessary lift?

One morning, the town looked like something from a Wilkie Collins melodrama, covered with a thick, autumnal fog. There were none of the familiar gulls on the tiled rooftops balancing on the chimneys – they had all chosen to fly off and float on the sea some distance from the long beach, adapting to the weather.

Very soon after that, I woke one day and realized my concerns about how to take off in a new direction didn't matter. The important thing was to leave and, with a startling newly discovered clarity, I was convinced that it was right, indeed essential, to explore the possibilities that must surely exist in another life.

Black Coffee

It's one of life's small mysteries how, when generations managed perfectly well drinking caffeine at night, suddenly it became the potion of the Devil as far as sleep is concerned.

The ceramics department of London's Victoria & Albert Museum houses a wonderland of porcelains and earthenwares. Situated on the top floor, far from the crowded entrance hall, paid exhibitions and shop, the collection features dishes, cups, plates and decorative ornaments from around the world. They're displayed in huge glass cases in the centre of the room, so that it is possible to walk around them as I did in search of coffee pots, curious to see how they had changed, if at all, throughout the centuries. What might they tell me about the practice of coffee drinking that is so much a feature of my day?

Back home, a slim wooden shelf in the kitchen houses my own coffee cups. Elsewhere in the room is the usual ragtag household collection – some random gifts or freebies such as the Ralph Lauren Stars and Stripes mug I was not entirely thrilled to see recently in a photo, plonked on the table Jeffrey Epstein was sharing with Andrew Mountbatten Windsor (once a prince) and Peter Mandelson. There are a couple of mugs made by a child in a pottery class as entertainment one wet afternoon and the odd expensive one, glazed in earthy hues, from a farmer's market or local potter. But the ones that I use every day for my black coffee are on that one shelf.

There are five small mugs my son gave me one Christmas, in a delicate off-white glazed porcelain with an indigo trim at the rim. Then there are six more, also a present, given recently by my sister. They too are small and in array of bright hues – moss, tangerine, nursery blue – all in graded colour with a white interior. They are all the perfect size for the many cups of black coffee that launch my day and that punctuate activity in the same way that cigarettes do, or used to, for other people. It's hard to imagine a life that doesn't include the coffee that has become so deeply embedded in my day. From a selection of various Bialetti stovetop coffeemakers that bubble up on the hob a couple of cups are poured for breakfast, and more over the next few hours. A telephone call embarked upon deserves a coffee. A telephone call completed is cause for another. Returning from a visit to the nearby shops for supplies is always time for a coffee. Taking one of my cups of coffee over for a chat with my next-door neighbour is often in order. After a few hours, if there is any left, it needs to be reheated in a small metal jug, something no coffee purist would ever do. And all of it black.

I remember when I began to take my coffee black, not as a shot of espresso after a meal, but as daily fuel. I was sitting in the basement of a house off the King's Road, where the nutritionist Petronella Ravenshear held her consultations. At that time, I was feeling particularly exhausted and overweight and Calgary, a lithe Amazonian member of the *Vogue* staff, recommended a visit to Petronella.

Usually, nutritionists hold about as much appeal to me as long walks, but Petronella's words resonated. Along with minimal carbs, protein balls and gallons of water, a key recommendation was to stop drinking milk in my coffee. No matter if it was skinny cappuccinos (and this was before the questionable introduction to the world of flat whites), milk would just be adding on the pounds. Coffee was to be drunk black. I lasted on the carbs and the water for a few months and then reverted to type, but strangely, the one edict I have embraced ever since then is black coffee. Occasionally, I will allow myself to order a cortado or macchiato, where the milk lies atop the thick black liquid and doesn't actually sully it – but generally, black coffee has become my beverage of choice.

Although the British are regarded as a nation of tea drinkers, proudly packing their own Twinings and PG Tips tea bags in their luggage and considering a nice cup of tea as a panacea for all manner of upset, coffee was the preferred drink until Victorian times. It had spread through the Mediterranean trade routes to reach northern Europe by the 16th century, but only made its mark in Britain more than a century later. The coffee houses that grew up were like clubs, places where different professions in London might meet – the military, scientists, lawyers, writers. Coffee was associated with debate, discussion and a certain degree of intellect, but only a certain degree, since such places still excluded women.

Yet something of that original clubbiness still hovers about coffee. Even an element of elitism that is missing from the cup of tea regarded by others as just as essential to their existence. But with a difference. There is a social element to the idea of the drink. 'Let's meet for a coffee,' people say, not, 'Let's meet for a tea.'

The appeal of the idea of drinking coffee, rather than the actual taste of it, is still a reason for its popularity. The veneer of sociability and even just a touch of sophistication is one of the factors that's allowed Starbucks to flourish. This company, where the coffee produced bears only minimal resemblance to what many of us think of as coffee and where you can buy a travesty of the drink like a cinnamon-laced frappuccino from one of their 44,000 branches, continues in its relentless march across the world. Not because we love the coffee they produce, but because we like to think of ourselves as coffee drinkers and they are always just there.

Coffee rituals are culturally ingrained, and become just as much part of the drink as the actual drinking. If, for example, you stand at a café counter in Italy after lunchtime and order a cappuccino or some kind of milky coffee, it's obvious from the owner's dismissive shrug that you are a philistine. In a recent 'Thought for Today' item on BBC Radio 4, Sughra Ahmed, a regular speaker on faith and communities, used coffee as an illustration of the stoicism that societies can demonstrate in even the hardest times. 'Cities still wake up to make coffee by the sea,' she announced – an excellent summation of the endurance of coffee as a social habit, even in many of the war-mangled cities of the Middle East.

And there are endless personal rituals. Some swear

that the slow drip through a paper filter provides the best taste and anything else is a travesty. Others prefer the French cafetière, letting the grinds steep before plunging them down. There are coffee fiends who have a master's degree in roasts and can explain at length the differences between Guatemalan and Colombian beans. There are some who are horrified at the idea of using pre-ground beans at home and insist every morning on grinding them freshly. Whatever the method, as the young Colin Wilson wrote in *The Outsider*, his 1956 bestselling exploration of alienation, 'The promise offered in the smell of coffee brewing is never quite delivered in the taste.' But that doesn't really matter. That promise is so good.

In the 1970s, I worked for a short time in New York in a midtown public-relations company. As with many New York offices, lots of the small rooms were internal, with no window, and one of these housed the coffee machine. I had never seen one of these machines before, where the ground coffee – not instant – dripped from the water container through a filter paper into a jug where it was then left to stew for far too long on a hotplate, before the jug was finished and a passer-by would refill the water container and replace the filter, piled with more coffee.

At the time, this was just as exotic to me as the fax

machine installed in another ferociously air-conditioned internal space with its near miraculous ability to send a replica document anywhere in the world almost instantly by dialling a telephone number. I would walk around the office with my mug of coffee – there was a stock of grubby china mugs on hand – wearing my second-hand Hawaiian shirts, handing out the faxes that came into the various addressees. Occasionally, if I was thought competent enough, I was allowed to send one. More often, I was asked to attend to the coffee machine. Some, and I include myself, think that American coffee has not improved tremendously since that time.

Like most homes during the 1960s and '70s, we always had a jar of Nescafé in the kitchen cupboard, but when visitors came, our mother would serve fresh coffee, in a blue and white Spode china jug, part of a set with matching cups and saucers. If there was a dinner party, which there hardly ever was, she served coffee at the end of the evening. Many households then had collections of exquisite small coffee cups for this purpose, frequently decorated with some kind of chinoiserie motif.

Now it's possible to snap up a set of these cups for next to nothing. Nobody serves coffee after dinner, which might be considered one of the small steps towards the disintegration of civilized entertaining. For years, people drank coffee after their evening meal, perhaps accompanied by a brandy, without obsessing about how it would disturb their sleep. In restaurants, it was completely usual to order a cup of coffee to finish the meal. And not decaffeinated coffee, which to true coffee drinkers is as pointless as a fake Gucci handbag. Simply nothing to do with the real thing. It's one of life's small mysteries how, when generations managed perfectly well drinking caffeine at night, suddenly it became the potion of the Devil as far as sleep is concerned.

Just before Christmas, I was trawling Portobello Market in search of gifts and saw a beautiful coffee jug on one of the tables on the pavement. It was right at the back of the table, a little hard to reach, painted in a deep-pink and green floral pattern. I wanted to buy it for someone, but who? Who serves coffee in coffee pots now? In the end, I decided it would just add another piece of unused clutter to a shelf.

After all those centuries of coffee pots in the Victoria & Albert, after the unglazed 18th-century earthenware jug, the 1760 enamel Chinese pot with a mythological creature's beak to pour from, the astoundingly contemporary-looking abstract design of a Spode pot from around 1830, the famous flying geese of a 1960s version, and the 1930s Susie Cooper Kestrel set, will there be any coffee pots to add in from the 21st century? Or, despite the huge variety of coffee available now anywhere in the world, will our contribution to the artefacts of rich black coffee have been reduced to a recyclable cardboard mug?

In Love and Other Stories

He made me into a construct of his dreams and I was as intoxicated by that vision of myself as I was by him.

Love is shapeshifting and uncategorizable. So many different kinds of love exist. There is a multitude of individual manifestations of this emotion we assume to be a defining element of being human. The achingly intense and terrifying love we have for our children, the love – maybe quieter but nonetheless intense – for the person we have spent years of our life with. Our love for our family, and even for our pets – a love I only really discovered I had when our cat Coco died last year. But when I think about love, it is that heady, delicious, sometimes reckless, sometime agonizing sensation of being in love that fascinates me.

In love. Where exactly is that place that we go to? Conditions divide between those we can be *in* – love, despair, need – and those which are equally powerful, such as guilt, envy, anger, joy, but that we don't inhabit in the same way. 'How many times have you been *in love*?' we might ask someone with curiosity mixed with voyeurism. Or we could ask that question of the person we are in love with, absolutely live with apprehension, jealousy and the fear of learning that they might have ever felt something similar about someone else to the possessed way we currently feel about them.

When people talk about being in love, I always remember a scene. It was sometime in the 1980s and it wasn't me who was in love. A close friend was weeping inconsolably in her West London flat one evening. She was desperate. Her boyfriend had left her out of the blue. He was a new boyfriend and they hadn't been involved with each other for long at all. In today's dating landscape, the relationship probably wouldn't even have been classed as exclusive.

Yet she was in agony. It was possibly the first time I had ever seen her cry about a man. In a gap between the tears she asked, 'I think because the pain is so great it must mean I love him? Well, wouldn't you?'

As it happened, I didn't think that, but I didn't say so. I wasn't sure I thought pain was the central indicator of being in love, but also nothing about the way she had spoken about him, previous to that night, had indicated such a powerful feeling. But she was experiencing rejection in a way she hadn't before, since it was usually her to be the one walking out. Her way of interpreting such misery was that it must be love. Only love could be so painful. And I did recognize that.

Love, while not in itself painful, opens the possibility of pain. If you don't want to take that risk, then you probably don't want to love – although how much of that is under our control is a whole other thing. Many of us will remember times when we have been in love as times that were laced with misery and pain rather than the more straightforward contentment.

How many times have I been in love? Now there's a question. In my case, the answer fluctuates depending on the day I am asked. Sometimes I will count five times, sometimes only three. Sometimes we can recognize that we were in love even when we are no longer immersed in it. But sometimes, once that has dissipated and we have moved on to be in love with others, looking back, it's possible to think that it wasn't love. We were never in love. Or maybe not in comparison to how we might feel subsequently. Because despite love being immeasurable, it is possible to compare amounts of love. 'I was so in love with him,' I have heard myself say. Not just in love, but *so* in love.

At any rate, the number of people I have been 'in love'

with bears little relationship to how many men I have been involved with over the years, propelled by desire, affection, loneliness, excitement and sometimes just proximity.

In a notebook, I once wrote, 'He thought that if he said "love you" enough, he might one day mean it.' I have no recollection of who that referred to, but I recognize that all-important difference. 'Love you' as opposed to 'I love you.' I wonder if whoever he was ever did.

I know that I was in love at 14 with a boy I'll call Richard, a couple of years older than I was, with long brown hair and dark almond eyes. I know because I remember how the mission to be with him was my only purpose in the day and also that the relationship involved enough agony to qualify. Neither set of parents was particularly keen on our being together, and increasingly, we would find places to meet outside our homes. We would spend hours romantically lying among the tombstones in the graveyard of the local church.

When we were able to be in either of our homes we would listen to Bob Dylan's 'Lay Lady Lay' and 'I'll Be Your Baby Tonight' while struggling with my not being willing to have sex. At 14, I barely knew what sex was and I never knew whether he had ever experienced it either. Although he made clear the blame for us being in this unsatisfactory state lay firmly on me – it was my failure. I still have the many letters we wrote each other wrestling with this problem.

My next love was a much older man who lived in Los Angeles. I was 17 and he was a bear-like figure of 36. He made me feel as if I were somebody completely different to the person I was, a slightly dumpy schoolgirl, failing to get on well with her A-level syllabus and yearning for a different existence. Instead, for what now appears some incomprehensible reason, he saw me as a mixture of a romanticized Burne-Jones–style love object, a girl eager to soak up anything he might introduce me to and, I suppose now, someone with the patina of youth that can be so seductive to anyone starting to get their first, as he once wrote, 'intimations of mortality'. And in his gaze, I too was able to imagine that I was that person – compelling and beautiful.

He introduced me to new experiences: musicians like Joni Mitchell and Emmylou Harris and the poetry of Hart Crane; he bought me jet jewellery and vintage editions of Edmund Dulac fairy tales. We would cruise down Van Nuys Boulevard in his open-topped Porsche swigging from bottles of Mumm champagne in a brown paper bag.

He made me into a construct of his dreams and I was as

intoxicated by that vision of myself as I was by him. I still remember the thrill of the international dialling tone as I secretly telephoned him in his Topanga Canyon home from my parents' bedroom. After I had to return to London, every few weeks there would be the excitement of the page upon page of typewritten letters on his IBM typewriter which arrived in thick airmail packages, written, I strongly suspect, accompanied by copious lines of coke and swigs of bourbon. Letters clearly also disapproved of by my parents, who couldn't fail to spot them in that morning's delivery.

Looking back, the impossibility of the relationship no doubt fed both of our feelings in different ways. By the time I had left school and was old enough for any real relationship to be possible, his obsession with me had faded, but not mine with him. I was still in love. It was probably then that I learned that being loved is not a prerequisite for loving.

I still care enough about the other men I have been in love with not to be able to write about most of them. There was one I only really thought I was in love with once he had left me and I spent weeks wandering around the streets in floods of tears. In retrospect, we were never in love with each other. There was another who I fell for dramatically on a first kiss by a window in a Huguenot house in Spitalfields, unaware at that point that a very long-term, both wonderful and miserable romance had begun.

None of these are either of my two husbands. That love was and is different and most definitely another story.

Author's Acknowledgements

I am always impressed by how many people other authors thank on their acknowledgements page. My list is relatively small but just as heartfelt.

Firstly, my gratitude goes to Alison Starling at Octopus, who commissioned this book, a book that defies genre, which is well known to be a publisher's nightmare. She has been unstintingly supportive from the first mention of this idea throughout the whole process.

Her team have been enormously enthusiastic and endlessly helpful: Jonathan Christie, who as designer had to put up with the very long process of my finding a cover image that would suit; Chloë Johnson-Hill and Charlotte Sanders for launching this book onto the world; and Alex Stetter for overseeing many of the issues involved.

Eugenie Furniss, my agent, as ever was a stalwart from start to finish and understood what I was trying to do with this idea, as well as being an excellent editor.

I also want to thank my son, Samuel Spike, for his help in finding the David Park image for the cover, which is just perfect, and for listening to me droning on about the book for several years.

As ever, David, who even married me during the process, was my rock and kept me going through the many moments of doubt. He bravely stuck his head above the parapet as an early copy editor of several of the essays. I very much doubt I would have managed to complete the book without his encouragement. But I am very, very pleased I have...

While writing this book, I have drawn the odd phrase or thought from a number of books and songs:

Pulp's 'Do You Remember the First Time?'; Rachel Felder's *Red Lipstick: An Ode to a Beauty Icon*; Nora Ephron's *I Feel Bad About My Neck*; Lucinda Williams's 'Side of the Road'; Carly Simon's 'Alone'; Olivia Laing's *The Lonely City*; Justine Picardie's *Fashioning the Crown: A Story of Power, Conflict and Couture*; Simon Hopkinson and Lindsey Bareham's *Roast Chicken and Other Stories*; Sally Clarke's *First Put on Your Apron*; Arabella Boxer's *First Slice Your Cookbook*; *The Constance Spry Cookery Book*; Lindsey Hilsum's *In Extremis: The Life of War Correspondent Marie Colvin*; Mary Douglas's *Purity and Danger: An Analysis of Concepts of Pollution and Taboo*; Vincenzo Latronico's *Perfection*; Tolstoy's *Anna Karenina*; William Makepiece Thackery's *Vanity Fair*; Sally Rooney's *Conversations with Friends*; *Mrs Beeton's Book of Household Management*; Elizabeth David's *Summer Cooking*; Georgina Battiscombe's *English Picnics*; Steven Gundle's *Glamour – A History*; Joan Didion's *The White Album* and 'Los Angeles Notebook' from *Slouching Towards Bethlehem*; *Gigantic Cinema: A Weather Anthology*, edited Paul Keegan and Alice Oswald; Maria Kondo's *The Life-changing Magic of Tidying Up*; Zadie Smith's essay 'Can You Be Serious and Seriously Glamorous?'; Colin Wilson's *The Outsider*.

Grateful acknowledgement is made for permission to reprint excerpts from the following copyrighted works:

'Snow' from *Collected Poems* by Louis MacNeice (Faber & Faber); reproduced by permission of David Higham Associates.

Index